MW00416725

Best wishes!

Dave

What people are saying about Fran's Story:

"Just finished reading Fran's Story. It is a wonderful read and sure brings back memories of my grandparents' farms in Ohio and Alabama. And we think we are busy today! Fran's Story shows the remarkable inner strength of women and how every part of her revolved around the family and leadership in training children to become responsible citizens. What a legacy. The thing I remember most about your Mother was her cheerful dispositon and the bright smile that graced her face when someone stopped by to visit."

- Sue S., family friend

"I recently finished your very moving book about your mother and her "story." It brought back memories for me of not only meeting her but also that whole generation and especially my parents. I can't believe how much you look like her in some of the photos! Thank you for assisting in creating and disseminating such a wonderful tribute to Fran and your shared experiences. Tears came to my eyes when I read the portions about discovering the mince meat cookie recipe. I have experienced similar things and find great comfort in knowing that our mothers are with us."

- Barbara L., Friend of Linda's who knew Fran

Fran's Story

The 90 Year Journey of a Kansas Farm Girl

by Harriet Frances (Carey) Frazier
as told to Linda S. Thompson,
her eldest daughter

Copyright@2007
Life Path Solutions, Inc.
All Rights Reserved

No part of this book may be reproduced in any form or by any means, electronic or mechanical, including photocopying, recording, or by any information storage or retrieval system, without written permission from the author; except for the inclusion of brief quotations in published reviews.

ISBN:978-0-9764903-6-4
First Printing   January 2007

This publication is designed to provide accurate and authoritative information with regard to the subject matter covered. It is sold with the understanding that the author is not engaged in rendering legal, financial, or other professional advice. If legal advice or other expert assistance is required, the services of a competent professional should be sought.

- From a *Declaration of Principles* jointly adopted by a
Committee of the American Bar Association
and a Committee of Publishers and Associations

Printed in the U.S.A. by
Lightning Source Inc. (US)
1246 Heil Quaker Blvd.
La Vergne, TN USA 37086
1-615-213-5815

In Loving Memory

Harriet Frances (Fran) Carey Frazier

December 15, 1915 - January 26, 2006

Other books by Linda S. Thompson:

Planning for Tomorrow, Your Passport to a Confiden tFuture

A Caregiver's Journey, You Are Not Alone

Building Your Safety Net for Life (workbook)

Table of Contents

Introduction 1

Chapter 1, Looking Back 5

Chapter 2, The Road West – Before my Time 7

  My Father's Journey to Kansas 7

  Mother's Journey to Kansas 8

  Mama Learned to Quilt 11

  The Courtship of Mama and Dad 12

Chapter 3, Daily Life When I Was Young 15

  Time for Butchering 16

  Churning the Butter 18

  Doing the Laundry 19

  A Clean House 21

  Family Life 22

  The Little Red School House 23

Chapter 4, The Neighborhood 31

  In The Kitchen 33

Chapter 5, Home On The Range 39

  The River 40

  Kin Folk 42

Chapter 6, Home For The Holidays 49

  All Decked Out 50

  There's No Place Like Home 52

  It Pays To Be "The Baby" 55

  Hobbies 56

  High School 57

Fran's Photo Album 61

Chapter 7, The Great Depression 77

  The "Dirty Thirties" 78

  Quilting as a Way to Pass Time 79

Table of Contents (continued)

The Grasshopper Invasion 81

Earning A Living 82

Chapter 8, Dating And Marriage 85

The War Years 87

Visiting New York City 89

Dad and "The Boys" 89

The Loss Of The Farm 90

The Train Accident 91

Chapter 9, Having A Family 93

Back to the Farm 94

Music in The House 95

Family Life 96

The Dairy Farm 98

Chapter 10, Moving To The City 99

On the Move Again 100

Life as a Widow 102

I'm a Grandma! 103

A Trip I'll Never Forget 104

Chapter 11, Harriet's Treadle Arts 107

One More Retirement 108

Some Final Thoughts 109

Chapter 12, The Final Chapter 111

How is a Mother Remembered? 116

Fran's Favorite Candy Recipes 117

Fran's Recipe for Chocolate Fudge 117

Fran's Recipe for Divinity 118

My Wish For You 118

Fran's Family Tree 119

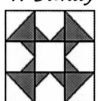

A Dandy

Introduction

On January 26, 2006, Harriet Frances Carey Frazier, my beloved Mother, began her journey to eternal life. We had shared a home since 1994, and she passed as she wanted – quick, pain free, in her own home, in her own bed. But more on that later.

At the grand old age of 78, she retired from her third career and moved from Denver to be with me in Phoenix. After a year or so of fixing up our new home and getting her gardens worked and planted, she was bored. Thus began this story. I asked her to write her memoirs because I do not believe that any generation before or after will see the changes those of my Mother's generation have seen. When they are all gone, if we have not preserved the stories, how will we know where we came from and who we are?

Mama was a good writer, although she would deny it. She wrote this story in long hand, and I would key it into my computer, print it out, and we'd edit it together. Add, change, embellish – I was always asking questions, wanting more information. Many times I would hear her say, "No one is going to care about the details." I'd respond with, "I care." That seemed to be enough, and she'd write some more.

Once the manuscript was done, she spent weeks going through old magazines, tearing out pictures of some of the old farm and kitchen equipment, or other things that would help you readers gain a visual perspective of how she lived. I've also taken the liberty of including a lot of family photos because this book is, after all, Fran's story.

The footnotes are as I remember her telling the story to me, or as I personally experienced it. My sister and I have said many times that Mama was born into the wrong generation. She was as independent as could be and although I know she and Dad loved one another, I am not convinced she would have chosen marriage and family had she been born 50 years later. After my Dad passed in 1969, she had two social dates, something my sister and I encouraged. After trying it twice, she loudly proclaimed that she wasn't interested, and went on to live 37 more years making her own decisions and charting her own course. She was never afraid to say what needed to be said, to do what needed doing, and definitely not hesitant to say it or do it in her own way.

As she got older, she approached the end of her life on this earth in the same pragmatic way she had approached everything else. When we were going over some documents stating her wishes for her final days and for the last ceremony, I was amazed at her comment (in her own handwriting) that went like this. The question was, "If there is to be a memorial service for me, I wish for this service to include the following:" Mom's handwritten response was, and I quote: "I do not want a memorial service, but grave side services only. My philosophy is: if you didn't come to see me while I was alive, you don't need to see me after I'm dead." That was my Mama. In another section of this same document, it asks about end-of-life medical decisions. Once again she said, "I do not want to have artificially administered food and fluids for the purpose of keeping me alive. I do not want to be on life support. My philosophy is, when it is my time to die, then let me die."

Because quilting was one of her passions in life, her story refers a lot to the art of quilt making. I mentioned previously that she retired from her third career to relocate to Phoenix. That third career was managing my sister's quilt shop in Denver. They had started this business in a very little old house, and within ten years had built it to be the premier quilt shop west of the Mississippi River. Not bad for someone who had *retired* after twenty years working for a major manufacturing company in Denver.

The front cover of this book is the last full sized quilt Mama made. She hand-appliquéd and hand-quilted every stitch. It was her swan song, her piece d' resistance. It is exquisite, and has now been added to my sister's collection.

The back cover is a photo I took of her in the mid-1990s. I came home from work one evening and she was sewing up a storm. This was during the conflict in Yugoslavia. The babies and little children of Kosovo were constantly in the headlines and on the news shows. I asked her what she was doing and she said, "I've been watching the news about those babies in Kosovo. My heart aches for them and no little baby should be without a quilt." My Mother made fourteen baby quilts in two weeks. I found an organization that promised to get them to Kosovo, but before I delivered her labor of love to them, I took this picture.

This was my Mama. Her heart just broke when she watched the news about abused children, sick children, and those who went to bed hungry every night. We weren't rich, but she had a special fund set aside that she used to donate to organizations on behalf of the children of the world.

She was full of adventure and never one to back down from trying something new. She went cross-country skiing for the first time when she was 65. She traveled across the US and to Europe after she was 65. Her interest and joy at seeing and learning new things was an inspiration for me then and now. While Harriet and I were growing up, I don't remember seeing her ever taking time to read. After she moved to Phoenix, she became a voracious reader. When her sight was on the decline, I purchased large print books for her, and because she was no longer as mobile as she'd like, she devoured every book I brought home. She would read the newspaper cover to cover every day, cut out articles and say to me, "You need to read this."

Although she would say she was a loner, she loved having guests in the house and we entertained a lot. As her hearing progressively worsened, she had difficulty tracking conversations, but that never deterred her from trying her best. Fran was an amazing woman and my role model in so many ways.

I could ramble on for pages about my Mama, but I'd rather you read her story as she wrote it. I did not edit to make pretty, nor did I change her words in any way after she was gone. This story is what she wanted to say and how she wanted to say it. She would tell you she didn't do much in her life; that she didn't make a mark on society. Those who knew her and loved her would disagree. She was a beautiful lady, a true inspiration to many and the world is a bit less bright without her smile.

A Scrap Patch

Chapter 1
Looking Back

My back aches as I put the last stitches in the Sunbonnet Babies quilt. Leaning back, I feel a sense of satisfaction, but I also sense anticipation as I look forward to my next project. I can't recall how many quilts I've made in my lifetime, but neither can I recall a time when quilts were not a part of my life.

Having recently celebrated my 82nd birthday, I wonder how many more quilts are in me. As I stitch away in the evenings, my daughter, Linda, often questions me on my life – how I used to live, what we used to do, and what changes I've seen over the years. This is the story of my life and how quilting has woven a tapestry through it. It started out as a family history for my granddaughter, but evolved into a book I hope will bring to readers a sense of what life was like before television, the walk on the moon and the Internet.

In my eighty plus years of life, I have seen many changes take place; some good and some perhaps not so good, depending on how one values things. It is remarkable what you remember of your childhood and days of youth. I have tried my best to describe life as it was, the type of tools we had to work with, and the general living conditions. My family was one of thousands of hard working men and women who made their living off the land. I have always felt it important that current and future generations understand how their ancestors worked and lived. Our lives were full and happy, even without the taken-for-granted conveniences of today, and I do not believe we suffered for lack thereof.

Bear Paw

Chapter 2
The Road West – Before My Time

Kansas. What do you think of when you hear that word? Rolling plains? Golden fields of wheat? The Wizard of Oz? Or perhaps just the middle of nowhere? Everyone's imagination takes over at the word, but in fact, it's a little of all these things. I remember my father telling us stories of his journey to his final destination – Kansas.

My Father's Journey to Kansas

I was born the eighth, and last, daughter of a well-respected farm family. My father, Frank Carey had migrated west from Green County, Pennsylvania at age twenty-one. He had been left an orphan at age four; his mother died in 1873 when Frank was two. His father was killed in a grist mill accident in 1879 when he was four. His Grandmother Cary raised him until she could no longer care for him. His Uncle Elias then took Dad into his home, where he lived until he finished high school. Uncle Elias wanted Dad to attend college in Waynesburg, Pennsylvania, but like most young boys, Dad opted for adventure and headed west where Uncle Charley, his mother's brother, had settled several years before.

The family name was spelled Cary, but when Dad moved to the farm he purchased near Downs, Kansas, there was another Cary family in the area. The mail was constantly getting mixed up, so Dad added the "e" to his name; hence our family name became Carey.

I remember my father talking to me of his trip from Pennsylvania to Kansas. He was traveling by train to a strange and unfamiliar part of the country. His train reached Chicago, and discovering he had several hours layover, he decided to take in a few sights around the city. He had not had much to eat on the trip thus far, so seeing a hustler selling hot tamales from his push cart, he decided to try a few. He purchased several and devoured them. Later, he came upon another bargain he could not pass up – bananas. He wished though, after consuming so many of these delights that he had been more cautious, as the combination of the two made him very ill.

Dad arrived in Kansas at his Uncle Charley Guttery's farm near Alton. He and Aunt Vic (Victoria) welcomed him with open arms and this was where he made his home until he met and married Elizabeth (Lizzie) Fuller in 1892. The young couple returned to Pennsylvania and gathered the household furnishings that had been willed to Dad

by his mother before her death. They returned west and stopped in Kansas City, Missouri to reside there for a while. Being unable to find suitable employment, he returned to Kansas and purchased 160 acres of land, which became the family home for nearly fifty years. Dad was a hog breeder for many years until the hog market collapsed. Then he turned to farming corn, wheat and sorghum.

Plowing the Field

One child was born to Frank and Lizzie, a daughter named Hazel. Lizzie contracted tuberculosis, which was quite common in those days. She died in 1898 at the age of 27, leaving Dad with a small child to raise. Hazel lived with her Grandmother Fuller until she was five years old. Dad got so homesick for his little girl, he took her to the farm and hired a neighbor girl, Harriet (Hattie) Williams, to care for Hazel through the day while he worked the farm.

Mother's Journey to Kansas

William Henry Harrison Williams was born February 15, 1841 in Tennessee. He enlisted in the Union Army in Ottumwa, Iowa on October 1, 1861, at the age of 20. He was nearly blind in one eye due to an accident as a child. At the time he enlisted, he was questioned about his eyesight, but he insisted he could see equally well with both eyes.

In January 1862 he was seriously wounded and on January 2, 1863 he was honorably discharged. On September 17, 1863 he was married to Sarah A. Phelps in Ohio. In 1864, the couple moved to Iowa and a daughter named Ida was born there. In 1868, the family moved to a farm in Carroll County, Missouri near the little town of Rhodes on Turkey Creek, their home until 1885. Three boys and a set of fraternal twins, Harriet (Hattie - the older of the twins was my mother) and Jane, born March 20, 1871. Mother grew up following the boys hunting, and fishing in the creek that ran through the farm. Wild fowl were plentiful in the wooded area, and fish from the creek provided food for the family. Mama followed the boys and loved the outdoors, while Aunt Jane preferred helping Grandmother around the house.

Grandfather traveled west in search of a larger piece of land on which to raise his family. He purchased a quarter section (160 acres) in Osborne County, Kansas, west of the town of Downs. The place was occupied by the E. E. Easterly family. The agreement was made that the Easterly family would be vacated by the time Grandfather returned from Missouri with his own family. Grandfather went back to Missouri and told the family of his land purchase and that they would be moving very soon. The family started packing.

A wagon was covered with canvas to protect their housewares, bedding and clothing. The sorting began; what to take and what to leave behind. What few farm implements they could take needed to go in the bottom of the wagon. Household items, cooking utensils and clothing were packed in trunks and stacked along the sides of the wagon. An aisle barely wide enough to get through was left down the center of the wagon. This little aisle gave the family access to items needed when the family stopped for the night. The bedding was rolled up in bundles, tied and hung from the bows of the wagon cover.

Conestoga Wagon

The children were told they would have to walk and drive the livestock. as there was only enough room in the wagon for Grandmother and Grandfather, and he would drive the team of horses pulling the wagon. The children were required to wear heavy leather shoes, pieced together with rivets, not sewn as we know today. The day came when it was "Westward Ho", and the long journey began. Day after day, walking, stopping only when evening came and it was time to rest the animals and the family. A campfire was built, the evening meal cooked and sleep came easily. The next day was a repeat – over and over and over.

Hattie Williams came to Kansas with her parents at the age of sixteen. She, along with her brothers and sisters, walked along the side of the wagon and herded the livestock along the way. The heavy shoes the children wore created a problem for Mama. A rivet on her shoe created a bad wound on her big toe joint from all the walking and rubbing. This injury gave Mama pain all throughout her life.

The days were growing shorter, but the walking continued. Finally, in November 1887, they reached their destination. What a disappointment to find the Easterly family was still in the house and had made little effort to move. Grandfather had no choice but to pitch tents for his family and resort to the law to take possession of his home.

Mother and her siblings all attended the same country school that her children would eventually attend. Dr. Cross was Mama's teacher, and years later he gave up teaching to become a medical doctor. He retired from medical practice and moved to the town of Osborne. In 1939, Mama mentioned to me she would like to visit Dr. Cross, so one day I drove her to town to visit him. It was quite an experience to hear some of the mischief my mother had created, while her twin sister never caused any disturbance. An eighth grade education was all one could achieve when my mother attended school. College was very rare for children in rural areas, as it was considered for the more affluent families. Children didn't normally leave the family home until marriage.

Mama grew up as sort of a tomboy, and she continued to follow her brothers hunting and fishing. There was no running stream near the new home, so fishing was out of the picture unless they wished to walk about two miles to the river. This was for the boys only. Mama never gave up her love for fishing in a stream, and after her marriage she lived close to the river. Every now and then she would pick up her cane fishing pole and head for the river.

Mama Learned to Quilt

Treadle Sewing Machine

One special trunk contained Grandmother's sewing supplies, and a place was set aside for her sewing machine. Grandmother's sewing machine was a shuttle machine powered by a foot treadle. A wooden box sat over the machinehead when it was not in use. There was never a question that Grandmother's sewing equipment would be left behind. That was the only method the family had of having clothing to wear.

Grandfather had raised sheep in Missouri, and Grandmother spun her own yarn. Mama told of her getting in trouble when Grandma instructed her to do some spinning. She had been warned not to let the yarn run off the spindle or it would snarl up and become a "snotty nose" as it was called. A snotty nose was of no use, and had to be thrown away. Waste was not in my Grandparents' vocabulary. Mama apparently didn't follow instructions well, and the yarn went off the spindle. Mama knew she was in trouble. She took the "snotty nose" out in the orchard and buried it! Mama never told us if she was punished for her behavior. She kept that as her secret.

Grandmother saved all the scraps from her sewing and used them for making bedding. The wool scraps had to be pieced (the quilt pattern we call Crazy Patch). The pieces were laid out on a square piece of light weight cloth, basted down in any shape they would fit: then the edges were finished with fancy stitches of colored thread.

Mama learned this art and passed it down to her children. Piecing quilts in patterns came into the picture later, as fabrics became lighter in weight and more comfortable to wear. Cotton batting was used for bedding, and this added to the weight of the wool pieces, making bedding very heavy. Grandmother had a set of wooden pattern shapers. These were pieces used in tailoring men's suits. Shapers were used for shoulders and sleeves and other parts of a garment, as there were no patterns yet available, and a seamstress had to make her own. These shapers were stored in one of Grandmother's trunks and were handed down to Mama. Not knowing how they were used, the trunk was stored in the attic of the wash house, which burned to the ground in 1931. These, as well as many other treasures, went up in smoke that day.

The Courtship of Mama and Dad

Dad was courting Sadie Lockridge, a cousin of Mama's. One day, Grandmother and Mama were discussing this courtship, when Grandmother said, "Hat, I would cut her out if I were you." Dad later told me of a dream he had had. He dreamed that Lizzie came to him and warned him not to marry Sadie. Dad took this warning seriously and ended their courtship; thus the beginning of the courtship between Hattie and Frank.

Mama became the baby sitter for Frank Carey's small daughter, Hazel, for a year or more. On November 9, 1899, Frank and Hattie were married at the home of the bride's parents. Just before their marriage, a small four room house was built to replace the dug-out

A Dugout Home

which was the only dwelling Dad had at that time. I am of the opinion that this was a request of Mama's, as she was not interested in living in a dugout. A dugout was a cave – dug out of a bank with a roof over the top and small windows and a door at the front.

We girls used to tease Mama, asking her how long she and Dad courted before marriage, and her answer always was, "None of your business; about 15 minutes." Mama never lived that one down.

Grandfather Williams died February 10, 1900, leaving Grandmother and Aunt Jane alone. Mama's oldest bother, Uncle Bud, looked after them until Grandmother's death on July 19, 1904. This left Aunt Jane with no home. Uncle Bud took Aunt Jane to live with him and she remained there until her marriage on June 7, 1917.

Hattie was 28 years old when she took Hazel to raise as her own, and Mama was the only mother Hazel ever knew. Mama raised Hazel as her own daughter, and the family never considered her as a half-sister. Mama was a lover of children, and this was a blessing as she had eight daughters and no sons. My oldest sister was born in January 1901. I being the last, came along in December 1915. Hazel was teaching school at the Baker District, three miles southwest of our home.[1] She was rooming with Mr. and Mrs. Billie Crist, who resided near the school. Dad called Hazel to tell her of my arrival. Having been around from the start of this long procession, Hazel started to cry. When asked why she was crying, she replied, "Mama didn't need another baby."

Mama used to say, "I wouldn't take a million for any one of them, but I wouldn't give a nickel for another." Mother considered this her lot in life and bore her burden gracefully. Mama and Dad were proud of their family and provided a loving home for us. Not one of us ever caused them any trouble.[2]

---

[1] In the early 1900s, it was considered normal for a young woman to become a school teacher before marriage. Because the school houses were usually one-room, rural to the point of being desolate, and far from home, the teacher was invited to live with several hosting families throughout the school year. She would stay 30-60 days with one family, then move on to the next. Her room and board were considered part of her pay, as she was no longer a drain on her own family's resources.

[2] It should be noted here that Mother's home was very small in comparison to the homes we have today. It was a two-story wood frame house; three bedrooms upstairs, a kitchen, dining and living rooms on the ground floor. Grandmother and Grandfather slept in one bedroom with the baby when there was one. Each of the other two bedrooms had two double beds, and the eight sisters slept two to a bed. I remember the first time I visited that house, and thinking there wasn't much room for that large of a family. But Mama always said that it was the confined spaces that made them such a close knit family.

Clay's Choice

Chapter 3
Daily Life When I Was Young

The winters were cold and the summers were hot and sometimes very dry. Our water supply came from a never-fail well, pumped with the aid of a windmill, if the wind happened to be blowing. It was a rare day when the wind didn't blow in Kansas. A hand pump was the means of drawing water for household use. A pump handle was bolted to the plunger rod and the act of raising and lowering this pump handle brought water pouring from the open pipe, cool and refreshing.

Inside plumbing didn't exist in farm homes and a pail and dipper supplied our drinking water. The kitchen range was used for cooking

as well as heating. This stove had a flat top over the fire box and was the surface for cook pots, the coffee pot and tea kettle. The oven was in the lower center of the stove where the baking was done. The oven was also used for warming one's feet after coming in from the cold. A reservoir on the side of the range held several gallons of water. It provided hot water for washing dishes when the range was being used. One of the designated chores in the evening was to pump water for the following day and to fill the reservoir on the range.

Water Pump

The heat from the kitchen range warmed the dining room, where a large trestle table was stretched to a seating capacity for ten. When I was a child, each of us had a place at the table which was occupied by the same person at every meal. Babies started out in the high chair between Mama and Dad, then graduated to the right of Dad. Dad could then help them with serving portions of food. As the next child was born, each moved into the next position along the table. I never moved from my position

Wood Burning Stove

to the right side of Dad. I sat at this place until one by one, the older girls left home and the table was made smaller. Of course, I regained my position during holiday dinners when the girls would come home and the table would, once again, be stretched out to seat a family of ten to twelve or more. If chairs were in short supply, the seating capacity was increased by placing a four or five foot board between two chairs where three light-weight diners were seated.

At home when we were all around the table at mealtime, we would sometimes start giggling over some recalled incident. Dad let us have a good laugh, but when he thought we had enough time to get it out of our systems, he would use his knife handle and tap it on top of the table. This was the signal for us to shape up. Those who couldn't resist a few more giggles were sent away from the table until we got over our spell.

In those days, little children were never allowed to eat at the first table. Guests, Mama, Dad and the older girls were granted this privilege and I remember being very hungry before it was the "little kids" turn to eat. Mama always saved the water from the boiled potatoes, and I would put a bit of real cream in the water and have bread and potato soup to satisfy my hunger. This was often more appetizing than the cold mashed potatoes and gravy left from the first table.

I can't remember a time when we did not have a telephone. There were several local telephone lines and several families shared each line. We would eavesdrop (listen in on) our neighbors' conversations. We would also get the latest local gossip from neighboring families by listening to "cross talk," which meant that our line was crossed with another line and we could hear the neighbors' conversations.

Telephone

Time for Butchering

Butchering time was a big job at our house. This operation was started in early winter as cold weather was needed to cool the meat to prevent spoiling. There was no refrigeration as we know it now and we had to depend upon the weather. Our neighbors, the Becks, would join Mama and Dad and they would kill several hogs. After the animal was dead, it was hung from a pulley and dipped into a vat of scalding water. This loosened the hair which was scraped down to the skin, and then hung from a tree limb to cool overnight in the cold air. The next morning the chore of cutting up the animals into hams, bacon, ribs and so on began. The fat was trimmed from the ribs and other pieces to be cut up and rendered into lard, while the hams and bacon were prepared for sugar curing in brine. Sugar curing was coating the meat with a mixture of salt, brown sugar and liquid smoke, and packing these pieces into a large wooden barrel filled with salt water brine.

A clear day was chosen to render the lard. Rendering is cooking the fat pieces until they formed brown pieces of meat called cracklings that sank to the bottom of the kettle. The liquid was skimmed off and put into stone jars – this became the lard that was used to cook with. This was done in a large black iron kettle outside over an open fire. It took the major part of one day as the fat had to be stirred with a long handled wooden paddle constantly to prevent scorching. I was always sick after a few days of smelling the grease in the wash house where this butchering process was done.

The cream separator was in this same room, and twice daily we had to separate the milk in this greasy, smelly room. After the hams and bacon had cured in the brine for a certain period of time, they were hung in the smoke house, where a slow smoldering fire was maintained for several days. This was the final stage of curing meat. The meat was then wrapped in cheese cloth and stored in the cellar.

The wash house, located to the back of the main house, was a small building about fourteen foot square. On one side of the wash house was Dad's workshop and on the opposite side was the double-sided tub washer that was operated by a gasoline engine. In one corner was the cream separator, a machine which by turning a hand crank at high speed separated the cream from the milk by centrifugal force.

The cream was forced to the top and came out the top spout, while the milk ran out the bottom spout.

We always had outdoor cats to keep mice under control. And for many years, we had a shepherd dog named Trixie. After Trixie died of old age, we had a brown and white dog named Ring, for the white collar around her neck. I was very fond of Ring. One evening Ring crossed the road to go to the river for a swim. He was killed by a car and I had bad dreams about that accident for many years to come.

Churning the Butter

Cream was part of the family income and was sold to large creameries for butter production. The cream was delivered to the creamery in five gallon cream cans by automobile or horse and buggy. We would take the cream to town whenever items needed to be purchased for

the household. Mama would save out a gallon of cream, allow it to sour slightly, then pour it into a three gallon stone churn with a wooden dasher. We girls took turns stomping the dasher up and down until the cream turned to butter. If the cream was too sweet, it took a long time to make butter. The buttermilk was drained from the churn, and with a wooden paddle, Mama would work all the water from the butter. If any buttermilk was left in the butter, it would become rancid and unfit for table use. If that happened, it went in with the old lard for making lye soap for the laundry.

Cream Separator

Soap was made by melting the lard and butter in a large iron kettle over a hot fire, then adding the lye water before the grease got too hot. Lye is a product created by pouring hot water through wood ashes, creating a chemical reaction that was handled with the utmost care. If lye came into contact with your skin, it would burn and eat away the skin. Caution was the word of the day when lye was being used. If the grease was too hot and the water was poured into it, it would explode and create a fire. This mixture of lye water and grease was cooked until it was the consistency of thick batter; then allowed to cool and set. When cool and firm, it was cut into blocks for use in the laundry. Nothing can compare with lye soap for getting clothes white, and Mama was a fanatic for white clothes.

Doing the Laundry

Laundry was an immense job at our house. Mama would spend a whole day doing the washing, having started before we kids went to school and just finishing when we arrived home in the evening. Mama washed her clothes through two waters and then they were rinsed twice. White clothes were boiled after washing, and rinsed in bluing water to whiten them. Bluing came in two forms, liquid and ball. Mama always used the ball bluing; four or five little balls wrapped in a cloth and tied with a string. She knew just how many times to squeeze the bag into the water to get the right color of blue[3]. Mama never knew what "ring around the collar" or "tattle tale gray" was. Hand towels and dish towels were boiled for extra whiteness. A neighbor lady remarked once about all the white diapers hanging on the line saying, "Hattie doesn't dib-dab her white clothes." Mama took that as a compliment.

Mama used unbleached linen for hand towels. This fabric could be purchased at the dry goods store, as it was a common item used for hand towels. A piece of this linen was cut into long lengths and sewn together to make an endless towel. Our towel holder was on the kitchen wall. It consisted of two brackets holding a wooden roller which slipped through the towel that rolled the soiled towel away as it was used. I had a bad habit of standing at the kitchen door with my arm through this towel. Dad would say, "Get out of the towel," as he could visualize the brackets being dislodged from the wall.

Four lines of wire approximately twenty feet long were fastened to posts that had been set in the ground in the back yard. White clothes

---

[3] I can remember Mother using bluing in the rinse water for her white clothes. She inherited her love of white from her Mother, and dirty gray laundry was never seen in our house.

hung in the sun for bleaching, while colored clothes were hung in the shade to prevent fading. Clothes were gathered as they dried, and heavier clothes were hung last.

Mama had a clothes pin bag that looped over the wire of the clothes-line and slid along as the clothespins were needed. One time she failed to bring the clothespin bag in the house, and it hung out on the line for several days. There were always a lot of birds around the house and many house wrens made nests and hatched babies. One day, Mama went to the clothesline, placed her hand in the clothespin bag and discovered a mother wren had made a nest. Four tiny eggs were in the nest. Not wanting to disturb the nest, Dad took a tin can with the top open, nailed it to a tree limb close by and carefully transferred the nest to the tin can. Mother wren found her new dwelling, settled in and hatched four baby birds. It was great fun watching the mother feed the babies bugs and worms. Finally one day the nest was empty; the birds had taken flight. Each summer, the wren returned to nest in the same location in the tin can.

Monday was wash day and Tuesday and Wednesday were iron-ing days. Mama ironed everything she washed due to lack of space in dresser drawers and on closet shelves – ironed clothes took up less space. When I was too young to attend school, Mama would make me a bed on two chairs where I napped in front of the oven door, listening to the tea kettle singing on the back of the stove. Ironing was done with the old flat irons, heated on the wood range. Flat irons were a heavy piece of iron, polished on the bottom surface, with a detachable wooden handle that clamped on to the iron. These irons had to be reheated as soon as they cooled. There were always three irons heating at the same time. A heavy cast iron skillet was used to cover the irons while they were heating.

Flat Iron

Dad always provided things to make Mama's work a bit easier. He bought a gasoline iron for her, but she was so afraid of gasoline she wouldn't use it and went back to the old flat irons. These irons were certainly not what we have today. They were heavy; weighing between 1.5 to 2 pounds, so a full day of ironing was a very tiring job. I remember learning to iron. I started out ironing handkerchiefs. I burned my fingers a few times trying so hard to get the corners nice and smooth to do a good job for Mama.

A Clean House

Spring and fall were house cleaning times. Mattresses were carried downstairs to air in the sun. Bed springs and bedsteads were washed down with soap and water, and quilts and comforters were hung on the clothesline in the shade. It was a beautiful sight to see the colorful quilts hanging side by side on the clothesline. It was fun picking out the pieces that were scraps from our dresses. We wore mostly dark colored dresses to eliminate as much washing as possible. The fabrics were mostly shades of blue, dark reds and browns. Most of these older quilts were simple blocks, many nine-patch, simple stars and stripes. The fabric was called calico or wash goods, and few variations of color were available.

During the cleaning process, the rag rugs were taken up from the floor, ripped apart, and washed. The rag rug strips were woven on a loom and were about 30 inches wide. After laundering, they were rolled up and placed in a box until fall. The pine floor was then covered with a piece of linoleum for easy cleaning. In the fall, the cleaning process was under way again: the linoleum was rolled up, the floor covered with clean straw for insulation, the rag rugs sewn together again and carefully placed over the straw, then tacked down to the floor. Oh, how delightful to lie down on the soft clean carpet and smell the scent of fresh straw drifting through the clean rug.

Saturday was cleaning and baking day. The usual weekly cleaning consisted of scrubbing the kitchen and dining room floors, washing windows and dusting. Dusting was a never ending job as the wind blew day after day in Kansas. Mama usually baked bread twice a week. Two large bread pans, four loaves to each pan was one of the baking chores. Cookies, cakes, and pies were baked ahead for meals on Sunday and lunches for school the coming week.

Family Life

Dad got his first car in 1917, a Model T Ford with fold down top and brass lamps fastened to each side of the windshield. The lamps were oil burning and it is doubtful they pro-vided enough light for night driving, but they made the old Ford look pretty fancy. I think Dad had one of the first cars in the neighborhood. In winter, we would all pile into the car, small ones sitting on the older

Model T Ford

girls' laps. Dad had heavy lap robes made for the car and these kept the wind away from our bodies. There were no heaters in the cars, but side curtains made for enclosure were used to break the wind, rain and snow.

There were times when the roads were nearly impassable due to heavy rains or melting snow, but rain or shine, the mail was delivered every day. The Model T had been stripped of fenders, equipped with heavy chains that left deep ruts in the road where water from melting snow would collect and freeze overnight. We walked to school on cold mornings wearing four-buckle overshoes to protect our shoes from the mud. It was great fun to crush the ice in those ruts in the road.

My father served as County Assessor for a number of years and later served on the Board of County Commissioners for several terms. He was instrumental in providing the county with the first hard sur-faced roads. This was accomplished by using crushed limestone on the roadbed, and when wet and packed, it became very hard. Many times we left the car at the county road and walked home to avoid getting stuck in the mud. That left the car on hard surface for Dad's trip to the county seat to resume his duties the following day. Horse and buggy were still used when roads were muddy or blocked with snow.

We were all raised to go to Sunday school and church, weather permitting. Early Sunday mornings, the air was so still and quiet we could hear the church bells from town. Each church bell would have a different ring. Their ringing was to alert church members that they had an hour before services began. Arriving at the church, we all piled out of the car, each going their separate way to attend Sunday school. The "little kids" went to the basement of the church for Sunday school. There we had our own music and Bible stories. Each age group had a teacher and she would have pictures to color and stories to read for the hour before Church services began in the sanctuary. After Sunday school was over, I would go upstairs to join my parents for the morning worship hour. I would seek out Mama and Dad and sit between them. I spent many hours studying the beautiful stained glass windows and the stained glass dome in the tower of the church.

Dad was a self-educated man. He read history books like some folks read novels. I can't remember when we didn't take a daily newspaper. The newspaper was delivered by our mailman, Nate Wells, and later by Harry Richardson, Nate's replacement when he retired. We eagerly looked forward to seeing the mail carrier coming down the road, and it was always a race to see which one of us could get to the mail box first. Nate Wells was a long time friend of Dad's and he was more friendly with the kids on his route than Harry.

Newspapers were the only contact with the outside world; this being before the invention of radio or television. Through the mail carrier's loyalty to his job, we were kept informed of what was occurring in other parts of the world.

Dad read the newspaper from cover to cover, and I was always glad when he came to the "funnies" (comics). I would crawl up on his lap and he would read Maggie and Jiggs, Mutt and Jeff, and the Katzenjammer Kids, which were my favorites. Reading was an important activity in our family and we were taught to read at home as well as in the classroom.

The Little Red School House

Our country school was one and one-half miles west of our home. We walked to school, cutting across the field when it was dry, reducing the distance by about one-quarter mile. Dad built a wood section in the fence so we could crawl through without tearing our clothes. We would meet the Owens' kids on the way and walk together. Meadowlarks were numerous and their sweet song was music to our ears as we walked to school.

Prairie Bell, District #8, was the place for education from first through eighth grade for all of our family. Prairie Bell was a one classroom building, with a cloak room at the entrance. a library, and a full basement. As one entered the outside door, there was a room where coats were hung and overshoes, if worn, were set neatly in a row. A shelf held all the lunch pails (usually half gallon syrup pails), and below the shelf were hooks for drinking cups to be used at the stone drinking fountain. It was the duty of two of the older boys to walk down to the Reece's (the nearest homestead to the schoolhouse) and draw water from their well to supply the drinking fountain at the school. The water was poured into a stone drinking fountain and each child had a drinking cup marked with their name that hung on hooks on the wall. Water for washing hands was warmed on the furnace in the basement. The bathrooms were the two-holer outhouse type, which was all anyone in the community had unless you lived in town. Not many city residents had the luxury of indoor plumbing either.

One Room School

Our school had a library, shelved and filled with books for reference or story reading. A huge dictionary was placed on an adjustable stand accessible for students of different height. World maps were also in this room and a globe hung on a rope with a pulley above the teacher's desk to be raised and lowered as needed for classes. A rope also hung in the cloak room that was used to ring the big bell in the belfry. If the rope was pulled too hard, the bell would turn upside down and could not be used. If that happened, someone had to climb the ladder and reposition the bell so it could , once again, be used to call the children to class.

I started first grade when I was four years old, and my first grade teacher was Ethel Kimball. Many years later, Ethel told of my first day of school. She had assigned seats to each pupil. First graders sat in the front row in small desks. When she showed me my desk, I said to her, "Do I have to sit at that little dabby desk?" Laughing, she recalled this incident each time she saw me.

The summer I was five years old, the church was celebrating Children's Day. This was a day the children put on a program for the congregation. One Saturday, the children were to meet at the church to practice for the program, and my sister, Mabel, was driving me to practice. The new National Bank was being built on the corner of Morgan Avenue and Blunt Street, the street we traveled to get home. A pile of sand was on one side of the street and a pile of bricks on the other, which left little room for passage. One of the workers had left a wheelbarrow in the middle of the street. Mabel, knowing there was barely enough room to pass through, asked me to look out to see if she was going to miss the wheelbarrow. As I stood up to look, the handle of the wheelbarrow caught in the spokes of the right front wheel throwing the car into the pile of sand. This jolt threw me forward, my head crashing through the windshield, resulting in a gash on my face. I remember blood everywhere and Mabel was crying. A gentleman (we never found out his name), was standing nearby and saw the accident. He rescued me and carried me to Dr. Felix's office. Dr. Felix made three stitches to close the wound. This same gentleman drove us home. My parents were very grateful for him bringing us home and were very upset at my accident. The following Saturday, the movie *Cinderella* was being shown at the town theater. I asked Mama if I could go with my sisters and her response was, "I don't believe you should go; look at yourself in the mirror." I couldn't believe it was me I was seeing. A horizontal cut from just below my right eye and over my cheekbone was covered with a dark scab. I was no longer a pretty little girl. I consider myself lucky that my eye was not damaged, and I have lived with this scar all of my life[4] .

There were big boys in the upper grades and, like all boys, an occasional fight broke out among them. One day when I was in the first grade, a feud between Fred Leonhart and Virgil Owens broke out, and Fred picked up the ball bat and started chasing Virgil. Fred had a bad temper and threatened Virgil, who ran through the school house, jumped out the back window and ran home. The rest of the day Fred sat at his desk with the bat across his lap. The teacher was as frightened as we kids were. The next morning all was quiet, but care was taken not to cross Fred Leonhart. He dropped out of the eighth grade, so the school bully was gone.

The school's basement was full-size with a coal-burning furnace. During school session, the teacher lived with the Reeces, whose home was about 100 yards from the school. On severe cold mornings, Jess Reece would go to the school and start the fire in the furnace so it would be warm for the students who had walked to school in the cold. Recess was time to get a little exercise and fresh air. Recess was 15 minutes long; then back to class again until noon and time for lunch. Lunch time provided us an hour of play, and we had good swings, a slide and a push merry-go-round. Baseball was for the older kids and most of the kids wished to participate. If there was snow on the ground, our winter recreation was playing Fox and Geese and other children's snow games.

Our teachers were all female. We never had a male teacher and I don't believe male teachers ever applied to teach at a rural school. When recess or the noon hour was over, the teacher rang a handbell calling us back to class. We lined up on the sidewalk in front of the school door and marched in one by one like little soldiers. We took our seats, and school was in session. The teacher had all eight grades, and at times there were twelve to fourteen kids in school. We respected our teacher and she expected the best from us.

---

[4] Mama was always very self-conscious of that scar. From the time I could remember, she never let herself be photographed on that side.

Morning exercises started off the day. The teacher would pull the piano out from the wall, play a march and we would march around the room one after the other. The windows were raised to let fresh air into the room. This got our blood stirring and we were prepared to start to work. First graders had their classes first. Then they were given busy work to keep them occupied. One by one each grade was called to the recitation bench to review the previous day's lesson. If answers were satisfactory to the teacher, she would give assignments for the next day, and the class returned to their seats to study. Occasionally one student would cause some disturbance, and he or she was required to stay after school and do make-up work. No one wanted to stay after school. This meant walking home alone, and then explaining to his or her parents why they were detained. The teacher was happy to give anyone who asked special attention to problems the student didn't understand. If a student had a question, he or she would hold up their hand; then the teacher went to the student's desk and gave help on the question.

Many times while walking through the field on the way to school, we would find clam shell fragments which seemed mysterious. Many years later, researchers determined there had been an Indian camp in this location. A dig was conducted, resulting in finding a few artifacts. It was presumed the Indians camped here, which at that time was the old Solomon River bed, and they were on the high side of the river.

There was a ditch at the edge of the field that drained water to the riverbed after a heavy rain. Devil's claws grew in abundance in this ravine. Walking home, facing the cold wind, this was a shelter and windbreak. My sister Rowena and I would sit down in this ditch and open up the dried Devils claws and eat the seeds. They had a sweet nutty flavor similar to coconut. We never told our parents about doing this until years later someone said these seeds were poisonous. This was our secret - we had eaten many Devils claw seeds with no ill effect.

When we arrived home from school, Mother was nearly always in the house. If she wasn't around, we would start calling for her and she would answer, "What do you want?" Our answer always was, "We just wanted to know where you are." After a snack of milk and cake or cookies, we would start the chores, each child attending to her assignment. By the time the chores were done, it was supper time. After supper and the dishes were washed and dried, it was time for evening homework. Dad always sat at the table with us to give assistance to any problems we didn't understand. When we finished our homework, we could play games until bedtime.

After dark, artificial light was provided by Number 2 kerosene lamps. I sometimes wonder why Mother wasn't blind with all the work she had to do in near darkness. Dad always managed to provide the latest improvements for lighting: First the old Rayo lamp, which was a

kerosene lamp with a circular wick that produced more light than the straight wick of a Number 2; Then the gas line lantern which Mother was terribly afraid of. Best of all was the Aladdin Kerosene lamp, that had a mantle and provided a nice white light. Electricity was non-existent in rural areas and Mom and Dad had no electricity until after they left the home

Aladdin Lamp

#2 Kerosene place and moved into town.
Lamp

The Barr family lived East of us and they had five kids. Mike Barr was a shiftless sort of person, never caring for his crops or livestock, and his horses were always skinny. They didn't have a car, but always used horses and a Surrey. In bad weather, they didn't make their kids walk to school, but took them in the Surrey. Sometimes we would ride to school with them in the morning. In the evening, everyone going East piled into the Surrey for a ride home. Grandma and Grandpa Barr were buried in the pasture along the roadside bordering their farm. It always seemed spooky to walk by their graves. In later years, their remains were moved to the Downs City Cemetery.

Dad served as clerk on the School Board for 35 years, resigning after I completed the eighth grade. He felt he had served his time and that parents with children in school should serve. It seemed only a short time after I completed eighth grade that the old District #8 was closed, and what few pupils were left in the district were bused to the Downs City schools. The old red brick, one room school house stood for a number of years, empty of children's voices and footsteps until it finally collapsed from neglect. It had served for years as a meeting place for families and friends at Christmas, when parents would gather to watch their children perform with great pride. My father believed music was an important part of school activities and a piano was part of the furnishings. Teachers were required to play the piano if they wanted to teach at District #8.

Music and dialogues were practiced by the students in preparation for the big night. A Christmas tree was decorated by the children and each child received a sack of candy and nuts and an orange, which was a real treat. I don't remember if we had a Christmas vacation during school. We started school on September 1 and were out on April 10. We were all helpers on the farm, and work started the last of April or first of May, so school had to be finished by that time or the kids would not be able to attend.

When in grade school, we had track meets with two other districts: Pleasant Valley and Bethany Center. Contests of sack races, three-legged races, and my favorite, the 100 yard dash. There was a girl named Etta who was the entry for Bethany Center. She was tall with long legs and was a fast runner. My Dad told me he would give me a dollar if I could beat Etta in the 100 yard dash - at that time, I had never had that much money and I was determined to collect that dollar. We lined up for the race and I took off and ran as fast as I could. I crossed the finish line first. Was I ever proud of myself! The silver dollar was awarded to me that evening.

The last day of school was the highlight of the school year. Teachers and parents came with baskets loaded with good things to eat. The sawhorses with removable table tops were spread out in the basement. Enough food to feed a small army was put out, with more in the baskets should the supply run low. That was the day when children got to eat first and eat all they could hold of things such as Jell-O salads, pies, cakes, fresh fruit, and other good things not common to our daily diets. This was definitely an occasion to look forward to. The men played baseball on the playground, while the ladies set out the food. When the feast was ready, the big bell was rung for all to come in to partake of the ladies' culinary arts. After dinner, the children followed their teacher upstairs for last minute coaching of our program of songs and recitations we were to present to our visitors. At the close of the program, children were presented with awards for perfect attendance, perfect spelling, and the like. A gift from the parents was presented to the teacher by one of the school board members in appreciation for her hard work and dedication to her pupils. This gift was usually a piece of china or glassware. My sisters who were teachers received numerous such lovely gifts.

My father was a firm believer in education, and there was never a question about our wishes to attend and graduate from high school; that was a family requirement. He provided us all with a vocation to make our way in the world after we completed our education and left home. I always liked school and I guess I was an average student. I was good at spelling and reading, but don't remember the other subjects. In my Memory Book, I still have some spelling awards I received.

Chapter 4
The Neighborhood

Summer evenings were spent playing catch, swinging, and going to the neighbors for an evening visit where there were always other kids to play with. Dad would sit out in the yard and read. If there was any dispute, he would settle it before trouble started.

We had a croquet ground that Dad had leveled and cleared of weeds and stumps. This was in the orchard in a space between the fruit trees. Neighbor kids would come to play croquet at our place.

As children, we had a blackboard that hung on the kitchen wall and many hours were spent playing "Old Cat" or "Going to the Mill" at this board. We had to make our own entertainment, and since there were so many of us, it wasn't a problem.

Back when I was a kid, neighbors visited back and forth quite often, especially on summer evenings. The Owens family lived southwest of us about a mile if you went by the road, but by cutting across the field, you could shorten the distance by about one quarter mile. There were five children in the family; three boys and two girls. I remember my Mama telling the story of one boy who died when quite small. His death was caused from eating raw wheat, which caused acute indigestion, and Fannie Owens was hysterical over his death.

Harold, the youngest of the family, was my age, and Mildred was my sister Rowena's age, so we spent a great deal of time together. There was turmoil in the family, and when family disagreements became unbearable, Fan would bring her children to our house and spend the night out of fear of Chet. I doubt that Chet would have harmed them, but he had an uncontrollable temper, so we never knew what he might do. Dad acted as a peacemaker for the family and would take Fan and the kids back home the next morning. By then Chet would have calmed down, so life went on as usual.

Harold and I were buddies though we fought like all kids. We would get into a fight on the way home from school, and my dinner bucket was a frequent weapon used on his head. Mama often wondered why my lunch pail was always bent up.

Rarely did a Sunday pass that Chet didn't happen to stop in at dinner time, and Mama always made room for one more at the already crowded table. Mama always felt sorry for Chet, as Fan was a real witch and refused to get meals for him. After a day's work in the field, I remember him coming home to a meal of stewed rice and milk.

Jess and Bessie Reece lived a hundred yards or so from the school house, so the teachers stayed with them for the eight months of school. Jess was a thrifty farmer, being the first in the neighborhood to use a tractor to replace horses for farm work. Bessie always had a "hired girl" through the summer, and it was usually one of us Carey girls. It was easy for Mama's daughters to get this sort of job, as Mama had taught us to cook, clean, and do all the necessary household duties.

When I was around eight or nine, Jess purchased the first radio in the area. We would spend evenings at their house listening to the "music in the air." This radio was a small sort of box with dials on the front and a large horn on top that served as the speaker. This was a giant step forward from the old cylinder record phonograph that we had. Bessie also had a player piano that was one of the most fantastic things I had ever seen.

Phonograph

When I was in second grade, Bessie Reece was entertaining the BY's social club for their weekly quilting bee. The hostess offered a bit of entertainment. Bessie asked me to sing the song, *Long Long Ago* for her program. I was dressed in a long dress with apron and sunbonnet. I walked in the room, sat down at the piano, found the right key and sang for the ladies:

Oh times have changed since we were girls,
Long, long ago.
We never wore our hair in curls,
Oh, dear no.
We went to bed at half past eight.
We never dared to stay up late.
Nor linger long out by the gate,
Long, long ago.

No doubt there was another verse or two, but this is the one that comes to my mind at this late date. When my song was completed, I rose from the piano bench, gave a little curtsy and returned to school - my first solo. I didn't take my eyes off the piano keys nor did I look at the audience. I was so bashful.

In The Kitchen

My Mama always raised chickens and a had huge garden. Mama hatched her own chickens by saving perfectly formed eggs and keeping them in the cellar. When she had several hens that were ready to brood, she would place 14 eggs under each hen. In three weeks, the eggs would pip and crack open and out would wriggle a wet, ugly little chick. The next day after the chick had dried under its Mama's wings, it would be a little handful of red, yellow or black fluff, depending on what breed of chicken she was. Home incubators were used in place of setting hens if one wanted a large bunch of chicks at once. A tray of screen about 2 by 2 foot square was placed inside a box. Water was kept in a container beneath the screen and a #2 kerosene lamp sat on the outside of the box to provide the heat for germination. Each day, every egg had to be turned. Mama marked an "X" with a pencil on each egg so she knew what eggs were turned each day. What a sight when she pulled open the door, slid out the tray, and there was a layer of fluffy, lively, peeping baby chicks. This is when we knew Spring had really arrived.

I loved baby chicks; they were so soft and fluffy. We would have a few of the first hatched in a box by the kitchen stove for warmth until the rest of the eggs were hatched. Then they were returned to their mama

hen. One night I sneaked a chick to bed with me by letting it run up my sleeve. Mama didn't know I had the chick, but found it the next morning smashed – no more chicks to bed!

Baby Chicks

We had a rather large orchard, so vegetable and fruit canning was a never-ending job for Mama from June through October. For many long hours she slaved over a hot wood-burning stove to make peach and apple butter that was delicious on her home made bread. The hot water bath method was used for canning and was done in the wash house. We used a 20 gallon boiler which held twenty to twenty-five quart jars at one time. Dad had dug a fruit cellar just outside the back door of the house, and this was the storage place for canned goods as well as potatoes, apples, home-cured hams and bacon, lard, cream and eggs. It was a cool place in summer and warm in the winter. Occasionally, there would be a lizard or water puppy in the doorway at the bottom of the steps, where it was damp and cool. As a kid, to me they appeared to be monsters that were just waiting for me to come down the stairs. To avoid seeing them, I would raise the outer door and slam it shut to frighten them back into their hiding place before I would proceed down the cellar steps.

The Root Cellar

My parents raised the majority of our food supply. When the ground was warm enough to turn, Dad hand-spaded the "little" garden, a patch about 50 feet square, fenced to keep the chickens out. The little garden was hand-spaded since it was too small for horse and plow. The ground had to be just right to have a good garden. If the ground was turned when frost was still in it, or if it was too wet, the soil would be hard and cloddy and would not be mellow and smooth for planting.

Dad planted lilac bushes around the east side of the yard fence and along the south side of the little garden to protect it from the hot south wind. This was a beautiful sight when in full bloom, as well as perfuming the area around the house with the sweet lilac scent. The little garden had two gooseberry bushes and rhubarb plants. Onions, lettuce, radishes, and peas were planted as an early garden.

The big garden was turned by means of a walking plow pulled by one of our most gentle horses. When I became old enough, my job was to lead the horse around the garden while Dad handled the plow. Then it was leveled by means of one section of harrow pulled by the horse. A harrow is a section of four rods approximately five feet long, joined together. Each rod contained steel spikes about four inches long. By dragging the spikes over the plowed ground, this broke up the clods and smoothed the soil. Beans, tomatoes, parsnips, beets, etc. were planted in straight rows made by stringing a wire fastened to stakes and measured a certain distance apart. Seeds were planted, covered and left to sprout. They put in an appearance in a week or so.

At the time, it seemed like we planted an acre of potatoes. Seed potatoes were cut into pieces with at least two "eyes" each. Dad would plow a furrow in the soil, and I would drop pieces of potato about 8 to 10 inches apart. As he made the next furrow, he would cover what had just been dropped. An undesirable summertime job was de-bugging the potatoes. Hard-shelled beetles would eat up the vines in a very short time if they weren't picked off. A pail of water with a bit of kerosene added was carried along the row, and the bugs were picked off the vine and put into this solution. That took care of the bugs. It was always an exciting time when Mama would go to the potato patch to look for cracks in the ground. This was an indication that there were potatoes close to the surface. New potatoes and new peas cooked together and thickened with real cream, was a most delicious dish to eat with fried chicken, our summer supply of meat.

When I was about four or five, I never sat still; always on the move. Mama had cautioned me never to dart in front of her when she was carrying food to the dining room table. One summer day, Mama had made a big kettle of gravy for the noon meal. As she was carrying this hot gravy to the table, I ran in front of her, grazing her arm enough to tilt the bowl, and hot gravy spilled down my neck. I was not seriously burned, but I learned a good lesson and never darted in front of Mama again.

My Dad introduced me to the hoe handle when I was quite small. I tagged after him everywhere he went, so he gave me something useful to do. He never liked weeds around the place, so there were several hoes hanging in places along the garden fence. I had no excuse and kept the fence row weed-free.

In mid-summer when the corn was ready to eat, we would pick sacks of ears early in the morning, take them to the house and lay them on the back porch in the shade. When Mama was ready, we all started husking the ears and cleaning off the silks. Mama would cut the corn off the cob, place it in large bread pans in the oven, add milk and stir frequently so it would not scorch. Then, the mixture was spread out on clean white sheets placed on makeshift board tables and left to dry in the sun. We kids would take turns shooing the flies away from the sweet smelling corn. When evening came , the corn was covered and sheltered for the night. The next morning the drying process continued until the corn was perfectly dry. Then it was placed in cloth sugar sacks and hung in a dry place for storage. This was one of our winter vegetables, because it could be easily stored and re-hydrated with milk when nothing was growing in the garden. The process of home-canning corn was not successful until much later.

When I was big enough to tag Dad everywhere, I became an expert at tearing a three corner hole in my dresses while climbing under barbed wire fences. Mama was not happy about this, so Dad started dressing me in overalls. I would never wear a sunbonnet as my sisters did, so a straw hat was added to my everyday wear. These are my gardening clothes to this day.

When the weather got so hot that milk and butter would not keep well in the cellar, we would place them in containers, set them in a shotgun milk can, tie a rope around the bale (handle), and lower them into the water well. A shotgun milk can was about 24 inches high and 10 inches in diameter, with straight sides, so it was easy to stack containers and retrieve them when needed for table use. Later, the City of Downs installed a power plant, and ice was frozen in 100 pound blocks that could be purchased for five cents per pound. Dad bought a large ice box, placed it in the cellar and kept fifty pound blocks of ice in it. These blocks had to be replenished two to three times a week, depending on how much was chipped off with an ice pick for mealtime tea or water. This eliminated using the well for refrigeration. A drip pan was set under the ice box to catch the water as the ice melted. Emptying the drip pan was one of the many little chores that had to be attended to daily so that the cellar didn't become damp and musty.

The Ice Box

Dad always planted watermelons on the sand patches where corn would not grow. Large dark green melons were a real treat, when chilled in cold water pumped from the well into the cement water-supply tank. They would float in the water, and when one had the urge to sample one of these melons, assistance was needed to pull them from the water to the plank cover of the tank. This was one delicacy that knew no limit. Melons were given to neighbors and friends. Dad never sold them, but would give one to anyone who asked to buy. Occasionally a group of unruly boys would plug the melons – then they would spoil and no one could enjoy them. Plugging was cutting a section out of the melon to test it for ripeness. We could always tell when this had been done, as the culprits would turn the melon over and the white side (the side laying on the ground) would show when the melon was turned over. This happened to us only once to my knowledge, and I think it was because Dad was not selfish with his melons.

Winter meals consisted of home-cured hams and bacon, and beef that had been butchered. Pork products were the mainstay of our diet, and the beef provided a nice change of pace. It was often that a hen was no longer producing eggs, and was killed for chicken, noodles and dumplings. Pressed chicken sandwiches were delicious in our school lunches. Fresh fruit was a rarity. Some of the apples we raised were stored in the cellar, and this was the only fresh fruit available. At Christmas time, fresh oranges were shipped in by rail. There were no refrigerated rail cars at that time, so cold weather was the only time perishable fruit could be shipped.

My parents friends', the Leaches, moved to Florida. After they had gotten settled, they shipped our family a wooden crate of grapefruit, oranges, tangerines and kumquats. Grapefruit, tangerines and kumquats were foreign to us, and we did not know how to prepare the grapefruit correctly. We were eating them like oranges, so we thought of them as sour and bitter. A while later the Leaches visited us, and the subject of the fruit was raised. Dad said he wasn't too fond of the grapefruit as it was so bitter. Mr. Leach told us how to fix grapefruit and it became one of our favorite citrus fruits in following years.[5] Kumquats were of little use except for jam.

---

[51] One of the first things Mama did after we moved into our new home was to plant a grapefruit and an orange tree in our back yard. For a few months of every year, she was absolutely delighted when she could step out her back door and pick breakfast off the trees.

Double V

Chapter 5
Home On The Range

When Dad built the house, a room about eight foot square was used for a pantry. This was just off the kitchen. As the family grew, a "lean to" kitchen was added and the old kitchen became the dining room. Clothes closets were non-existent in houses of that time. Mama converted her pantry shelves into storage space for the children's clothes.

Around 1905, when my sister Ruth was a baby, Dad "raised the roof" and added three bedrooms upstairs. Including Hazel, there was a total of five children thus far. Two of the bedrooms had two double beds and a dresser. Our parents' room had one bed, which became a guest room whenever needed. Mama and Dad used the folding couch in the living room as their bed whenever we had company. There were double doors leading from the sitting room into the parlor, and the parlor remained closed unless we had guests.

One of the bedrooms upstairs had a radiator where the stove pipe run through it. This was the only warm room upstairs and in the winter we dressed here. While preparing for bed we would sometimes get a little rowdy. Dad allowed this to go on for a short while. Then he would signal "bedtime" by using the stove poker to tap on the stove pipe. This meant our fun was over for the evening.

Dad bought a piano for family entertainment. My oldest sister, Mabel, learned to play the piano and many evenings were spent singing with Mabel accompanying us. My greatest desire was to learn to play the piano, but by the time I was old enough to take music lessons, there wasn't enough money for such extras. I learned to play by ear, strictly for my own entertainment, and I'm certain my parents wished many times I would give it up as a lost cause[6].

---

[6] I remember Mama playing the organ. She was a lot better than she would lead you to believe. There were few popular songs that she couldn't play on that organ

The River

The North Solomon River was the north boundary of our place. It was a peaceful stream which was shallow enough to wade in and set a fishing pole, in hopes one might catch a bullhead or a rare channel cat. This small river provided recreation for us as well as the neighboring youth. A large sandbar stretched for a goodly distance at the bottom of a sloping bank that was easily accessible from the road and directly across the road from our mailbox. Summer was wading time, with picnics in the shade of large elm and cottonwood trees that lined the river banks. To escape the heat, we roamed the river banks, but caution was the word. Poison ivy was plentiful, as well as horse weed, which made one feel like a hive of bees had stung you when it came in contact with bare arms and legs.

The North Solomon River was normally a shallow, low running stream fed by springs. During the summer, one could expect high water, due to heavy rains and run off, which usually occurred several miles to the West. The old riverbed was the best farmland we had, and we were fairly sure of a crop off this portion of the farm even if the upland didn't produce too well. Corn and feed would be six foot high one day; then that night a heavy downpour to the West would raise the river into a muddy, raging torrent of water. This water would oftentimes get high enough to run over the road on the low side of the riverbank and flood the river bottom, destroying the crops. As the river receded, most of the water would run back into the channel, but some was always left to seep away. This was a major inconvenience, as the milk cows had to cross the water to get to the pasture and we would have to walk around the high bank to drive them home at milking time. Dad fought an uphill battle all those years, fighting drought and floods at the same time.

There was what we called the "low water bridge" across the river east of our place. This was the road we used to go to town unless the river was up high enough to cover the bridge. During high water times, we had to go around to the county road to get across the river. A tragedy occurred at the low water bridge, which is still very clear in my mind. A man in the neighborhood was driving a team and wagon down the road headed for the low water bridge, and he knew the river was high. His son of about 14 was with him on this cold, cloudy morning, so they were wearing overcoats. This man attempted to swim his team of horses and wagon across the river, and when he found the current was sweeping the horses off their feet, he told the boy to jump. The boy's coat caught on the wagon brake handle and he was swept down stream and drowned. The alarm was sounded over the telephone lines and neighbors everywhere rushed to the river banks to search for the boy's body. He was found several hundred feet down stream, lodged in the trash along the riverbank.

There was another incident, not tragic, but not humorous either. A traveling salesman, driving a Model T Ford sedan loaded with his wares of penny gum machines and cases of colorful gum, crossed the bridge. His car lacked the power to make it up the winding hill on the East side of the bridge. He attempted to back down the hill and try again, but misjudged the edge of the bridge (which had no railings), and his car overturned into the river. He managed to get out of his car and seek help. Neighbors living close to the river brought their teams of horses, hooked onto the car and pulled it onto the bank. What a sight to see – all that colorful gum floating downstream wasted. Gum was a luxury we kids could not afford.

This same eventful place was used for baptizing new members of the Baptist Church, who believed one had to be baptized in a running stream. My sister, Agnes, was baptized there after she was married and joined the Baptist Church.

When winter set in and the river froze over to a safe depth, ice skating parties were frequent. We always had a huge bonfire burning on the sandbar to keep the skaters warm and to roast wieners and marshmallows over the hot coals. This satisfied the hungry skaters. It was a neighborhood party for all who wished to attend, and Mama and Dad were available should there be a crisis of any kind. To my knowledge, no one ever fell through the ice, as Dad was very cautious and checked the conditions of the ice before approving a party.

A hill in the corral provided a place to sled ride. Also, one could get a nice long ride in a coaster wagon, providing the driver could steer well enough to prevent an upset.

A small meadow just west of our house was the place to gather wild daisies. Just below the bank of the meadow was a shady glen that was covered with violets. On spring evenings, after chores were done, we would walk up to the meadow and return with violets and daisies in bunches as large as our hands could hold. We provided Mama with wildflower bouquets such as Indian Bread, wild Verbena, and perhaps the first blooming Sunflower. Even though the Sunflower was the Kansas State Flower, it was a real pest, and considered a weed to those of us who had to chop them out of the corn rows. But, they were still a flower, and picking them caused a sticky sap to run from the stem. This sap had a very unpleasant odor that remained on one's hands for some time.[7]

In 1922, my sister Gladys was teaching in the Pleasant Valley rural school. One of the older boys came to school one day and announced he thought he had small pox, a dreadful disease which caused disfigurement and sometimes death. The school was immediately closed, and all who had been exposed were under quarantine. Gladys came home, and Dad called Dr. Felix out to our house to vaccinate all of us. Dad was first. Then he took me on his lap and held me while the doctor gave me the shot. None of our family had the disease, and we were grateful, as the pox left ugly scars.

Kin Folk

Mama's twin sister, Jane, married late in life and had no children. She married Tom Anderson, who made his living by traveling around the country selling Raleigh products. His line consisted of spices, ointments, cleaning products, etc. He carried a sample case, and each

---

[7] I found this part laughable when I was typing Mom's manuscript. When we lived on the farm, she used to swear at the Sunflowers. When we moved into our Phoenix home, she planted Sunflowers in the back yard. Believe me, I teased her a lot about this.

time he came to our house, we kids gathered around Uncle Tom to enjoy the scent of unfamiliar spices that drifted from his sample case. He never forgot that we were "little kids" and always had a sack of candy for us. Mostly, he brought stick candy, and needless to say, we were very fond of Uncle Tom and Aunt Jane. They always spent holidays at our house, as they lived in Osborne and it wasn't convenient for Mama to take all of us there. One Sunday, after the older girls had grown to the point they didn't have to go with the folks, Mama, Dad, Rowena and I were spending Sunday at Aunt Jane's house. Being from the farm, city life was a real drag for us – nothing to do but walk up and down the sidewalks. Water lines running adjacent to the sidewalks had "manholes," a metal, circular drum with a heavy lid level with the ground. Inside these drums were the meters for checking the main line. This particular Sunday, Rowena and I were walking down the sidewalk and she stepped on a manhole cover. It tilted and she dropped inside the drum. She held onto the side of the drum while I ran back to the house to get Dad to rescue her. We were both frightened to death, as we had the idea that the hole was full of water and she was near to drowning.

In the summer of 1923, Uncle Tom and Aunt Jane were visiting his son in California. Returning home, near Simla, Colorado, Uncle Tom encountered some newly worked roads with loose sand spread along the roadside. The car skidded in the sand and overturned down a steep bank. Both were pinned under the car, but Uncle Tom was able to raise the car enough for Aunt Jane to crawl out, and he soon followed. A passing car took them to Simla, where medical aid was summoned. However, Aunt Jane's internal injuries were so severe she passed away that evening. Mama, Dad and two of my sisters were on their way to Missouri to visit Mama's old home place. Word reached them on their way. When told of Aunt Jane's death, they immediately returned home, where Aunt Jane's body laid in state at our house. Mama's heart was broken, and she never seemed to be her happy self after that.

Spending Sunday at Uncle Arnold's was punishment for me. Uncle Arnold was Mama's brother, and they lived in Downs, Kansas. I never liked Aunt Stella very well. She never smiled much and seemed like an old grouch. Uncle Arnold was lots of fun and was always laughing and joking. They had four girls - two were twins. They were all older than I, and the only games they knew how to play were "hopscotch" and "jacks," which had no appeal to me at all. I could only think of interesting things to do at home, like going fishing or swinging on the rope swing Dad had made for us. He had placed a metal rod between two huge forks in the box elder tree and tied a heavy rope from the rod. A 1" x 8" piece of lumber provided the seat for the swing, and had holes centered at each end to fit around the rope. Two of us standing on this board could pump and make the swing go as high as our courage would allow.

Mama had two other brothers, Uncle Gid and Uncle Bud (Ulysses), and another sister, Aunt Ida. Uncle Bud moved to California when I was quite small so I didn't know much about him. His wife, Aunt Della, died before he went to California. They had two children, Fred and Bessie. I can vaguely remember Uncle Bud playing the violin, and very little can I remember about Aunt Della, except that she seemed to be a very pleasant person even though she was a semi-invalid.

Uncle Gid was a funny guy - he had a big heart and was somewhat rough in his manner of speaking. I was always amused at his eating habits, such as eating peas with his knife. This was an art he seemed to have mastered quite well.

Aunt Ida was disliked by all of us, because of her hateful disposition. She married Jeff Wright, and I remember my Mama telling of the time Aunt Ida was making her wedding dress and remarked, "If I could see into the future, I wouldn't be making this old thing." Uncle Jeff adored her, but no one ever knew how she felt about him. They had a baby girl who died in infancy, and Mama always thought had the baby lived she would have been a happier person. Aunt Ida didn't like Mama's children like Aunt Jane did, and we never went to visit her as a family. She became ill and needed someone to stay with her, so naturally, she expected Mama's girls to accommodate her. This was a dreaded job for each one of us, as we took our turns. I was only about four years old at this time and I went with Mama to visit her. She was confined to bed at that time. She was a collector of "things." Someone had given her a little Kewpie doll made into a pin cushion. It was hanging on the wall just above Mama's head where she was sitting. I was on Mama's lap and I knew I wasn't to touch anything. I whispered to Mama to look at the doll, and as Mama looked up at it, Aunt Ida raised her voice saying, "You can't have that." That was the last time I saw her. I often wonder what happened to all her "things."

Uncle Gid was Mama's youngest brother. He was a happy-go-lucky guy. He married Pearl Edwards and they had ten children, although one boy died as a child. Aunt Pearl could waste more than Uncle Gid could provide. Mama used to give her bedding to keep the children warm when returning home in the wagon, but she never took care of anything. Soon the bedding would be hanging on the fence and destroyed. The family moved to Butler County, Kansas before I could remember too much about them. They would visit us nearly every summer, so it was always a jolly time when their family and ours got together. During the Depression, they moved back to Downs to care for Aunt Pearl's parents. The boys worked as cow hands through the summer, and in the fall they "rode the rails" to Colorado to work in the fruit, hay and bean harvests. Their earnings kept the wolf away from the door. Howard, one of the boys, spent a lot of time at our house, and he became the brother I never had. We were really close pals and he became a real buddy to Floyd, my future husband, before we were married. Howard went into the Army and served on two war fronts, reaching the rank of Captain. He made a 20 year career of the Army and died in 1988.[8]

Hazel, my half sister, taught school for a time after graduating from high school. She married Norman J. Reddick and they had one child, Lucille, who was just 18 months younger than I. I don't remember much about Hazel and Norm outside of the places where they lived. Their first home was several miles west of our place. One Sunday we were

---

[8] Howard was the only one of Mom's cousins who I remember. I can still picture him in his Army dress uniform and remember him as a tall and very handsome man who always had smile on his face and a ready laugh.

at their house and Norm started up the Model T to go someplace. Lucille and I got in the car and I was sitting next to the door. As Norm backed the car up, I went tumbling out on the ground. I wasn't injured, but thought I had been killed. Hazel and Norm then moved to the Ruby place, the farm joining ours on the south. There was a pond on this farm, and Norm would use the water tank as a boat and take us for a ride on the water. This was their home when Hazel came down with tuberculosis. She steadily grew weaker and was moved to Norm's mother's house in Downs to be near the doctor and Mrs. Reddick, who took care of her. When she was so bad, she wanted Mama to be with her all the time. Mama left her home and family to be at Hazel's bedside constantly. I remember the day she died. Our whole family went into town and one by one, we went into her bedroom to bid her goodbye. It was a sad time for all of us and I can still remember the look on her face as she told me goodbye. Hazel's was the first funeral I can remember attending.

Lucille was left without a mother at about the same age as Hazel was when she lost her mother. Norm had a brother, John, and his wife Bess wanted to adopt Lucille. Norm didn't want to give her up, so when he moved to Iowa to take employment in the Maytag factory, he took Lucille with him. His brother Bill and wife Frances took Lucille into their home, but soon tired of her and sent her back to Kansas. Bess refused to take her a second time, so Mama was obligated to give the child a home. She really didn't need another child to do for.

Lucille was my companion, as we were so near in age, but there was friction between us. My oldest sister, Mabel, always defended her in our disagreements because she felt sorry for her. I resented this, as I thought I should be considered as a sister. This caused hard feelings between my oldest sister and me, and for many years I still harbored this ill feeling. Lucille lived with us for about two years, until Norm re-married. Then Lucille went back to Iowa to live with her father. It nearly broke my heart when she left, as I had no one to play with. Even though we fought like all kids do, I knew I had lost my playmate. Norm died in February of 1936 of tuberculosis. Lucille married and had two sons. She died of heart trouble in 1990.[4]

.

---

[4] Lucille and her husband lived in Northern California. After our family moved to Denver, they visited us a couple of times over the Christmas holidays. I cannot remember his name, but do know that he and Dad always had a good time during their visits. Lucille had bright red hair (from a bottle, as Mom would say) and as a little girl, I was fascinated by this.

Chapter 6
Home For The Holidays

Holidays at home were always happy times for us. We were a close knit family, and with so many of us, there was always a crowd even without company. Sundays were the time for making home-made ice cream in the hand crank freezer. Dad was not one for ice "milk," like some of our neighbors made to save on the cream. Mother made the mixture of eggs, sugar, milk and cream, and I can remember the tiny bottles of "ice cream flavoring" that was used, and later replaced by vanilla.

Christmas at home was an event eagerly looked forward to even after we were all married and gone from home. There was nothing to take the place of us all going home for Christmas. When I was small, we always had a Christmas tree in the corner of the living room. It was brought into the house on my birthday, December 15, and evenings were spent stringing popcorn and cranberries and making red and green crepe paper chains for decorations. Real wax candles in tiny metal holders were clipped to the branches, but were never lit, as this was a fire hazard and many children's lives were lost from such fires. Each child received one gift, so we shared our gifts with each other. One day after I was grown, I asked my father how he managed to have enough money for all this, and his answer was, "If I didn't have the money, I went to the bank and borrowed it." We had our Christmas on Christmas Eve, and after we opened our gifts, we all piled in the family car and attended Christmas Eve church services. There were always some of us in the Christmas program.

My folks never taught us about Santa Claus. They had the idea this was being untruthful to their children. All my friends believed in Santa, so I thought I would find out for myself. I hung my stocking by the stove and the next morning I was really disappointed. My older sisters had filled my stocking with corn cobs and an old doll - proof to me that there was no Santa. I don't feel that we missed a great deal by not believing in Santa. We didn't know anything about the Easter Bunny or the Tooth Fairy or Trick or Treat. Those were city kids' activities.

At Christmas time, we were allowed to make lots of candy. We would make vinegar taffy, which was a mixture of sugar, water and vinegar cooked to a hard crack temperature. At this stage, it was poured into a pan and left to cool enough to handle. Then we would coat our hands with butter and pull the mass until it became white and glassy. It was then twisted into a rope shape and cut into pieces with buttered scissors. This was a project done with neighbor kids, as one's hands became very sore and tired. We also made fudge, divinity and a lot of other goodies. Chocolate fudge was my favorite, and this became my specialty. I still make several batches during the Holidays for family and friends.

All Decked Out

Clothing was a big item in our family. Mama did much of her own sewing, although she never liked it. Everything was homemade except for coats and shoes. Good quality coats were purchased so the next child could wear them when they were outgrown by the older ones. I well remember my first new coat. Dad took me to Cawker City, Kansas, where Mr. Rothschild ran a mercantile store. I remember Dad bargaining the shopkeeper down to where he could afford the coat. It was rust color wool trimmed with a light color fake fur. This really made an impression on me. I never thought about having to wear hand-me-downs or made-overs. I was just happy to have more than one change of clothes, which some of the neighbor kids didn't have.

When I got older and learned to sew, city families that we knew well would give us nice (but unwanted) clothes, and I would make them over to my liking. This was how Rowena and I got most of our clothes during our high school years. I never felt embarrassed by this; we were just thankful to have something to work with.

Our family had a lot of pride in our personal appearance, and we girls followed the fads that were the current style. My older sisters wore "dog ears." These were created by saving the combings from one's own hair and placing them in a "hair receiver. Then when we were ready to wear the dog ears, one would take a small amount of hair, make a ball and comb one's own hair over this ball. Hair pins were used to keep them in place. The ball of hair was placed back in the hair receiver to be used for the next occasion. I remember wearing "high buttoned shoes" when I was small. These shoes were about three inches above the ankle and could only be fastened with a button hook. When I was around eight years old, I had my first pair of new patent leather slippers. These were for Sunday wear only. Hat and gloves were in style, and one never thought of going out in public without them. In winter we little ones wore stocking caps. My first hat was given to me for Christmas by my sister Mabel, when I was around eleven years old.

July 27 was the town of Downs' birthdate. This was a big event for all the surrounding area. A carnival was set up in Railroad Park. There were baseball games for the men, and children could ride the merry-go-round, Ferris wheel and swings - all for a nickel each. I can so vividly remember the scent of the roasting hot dogs; oh, so mouth-watering. Ice cream cones were plentiful, but we were limited to one each.

The days started with packing baskets of food, dishes, silverware, iced tea and lemonade; and best of all, the quilts to be spread out on the ground under a giant cottonwood tree. Mama remained there on the quilts visiting with friends and neighbors, while her children scattered about viewing all the dolls, clowns, etc. to be given as prizes for winning some sort of game. How we longed to own one of these beautiful prizes. Back to Mama – time for lunch. Mama was standing under an umbrella when a lady ducked under the umbrella and remarked, "How many Careys?" Mama was never embarrassed about having a large family.

When I was about twelve years old, Uncle Gid's family was visiting us during the celebration. Maxine, their oldest daughter, was allowed to wear makeup, so she painted me up. When we went to the car to go to town, Dad took one look at me and I was told to go wash my face if I wanted to go. I was humiliated, but obeyed my Father's command.

There's No Place Like Home

I never would go home with other kids after school, but it seemed we had an extra at our table quite often. Home was the best place I knew. One Sunday, Mama, Dad and I went to Alton to visit Dad's cousin, Grant Guttery, and his wife. They had no children, and it was a terribly lonely place for a child. Grant operated a five and dime store and always had a supply of candy to hand out to us, and we liked him for that. His wife, May, was a strange person, and didn't know what to do or say to little children. I remember one visit when it rained that afternoon – that meant muddy roads going home, so Dad decided to spend the night. Even with Mama and Dad with me, I cried myself to sleep; I was so homesick. There was no place like home when darkness came.

Summers were long and hot in Kansas. After harvest was over, there was little in the way of green fields; just dry wheat stubble. The hot winds would blow day after day. It was not uncommon for the temperature to reach from 100 to 110 degrees for several days. We always looked to the West for clouds that might bring rain and cool the earth. Dad would sit on the cellar wall and watch for clouds in the West which never came.

Our bedrooms were upstairs, and insulation was unknown, so the beds got extremely hot during the day. We would sprinkle the sheets with water and let the dampness evaporate to cool the sheets so we could sleep in reasonable comfort. It would have been wonderful if we could have had some of that heat in the winter. Mama raised geese, so we had warm feather beds during the winter. Blankets were used in place of sheets, and quilts were piled on top. On many winter mornings we would awaken to frost on the covers from our own breath.

Dad would arise first, build the fires in the kitchen and living room, and then call, "Time to get up." We would run into the room that was warmed from the stove pipe and dress, then go milk the cows, while Mama prepared breakfast. Our breakfast menu varied from day to day. Pancakes, ham and eggs, fried potatoes, hot cereal, biscuits, steak and gravy; and of course homemade jam for the biscuits.

I was awakened mornings by the sound of Mama scraping the remaining dough and flour from the breadboard with the biscuit cutter. That was a signal that I should get out of bed, get dressed and go down stairs, as breakfast would soon be ready. As soon as the older girls had finished their morning chores, they would come in, wash up and we would sit down to eat. Early morning exercise produced hearty appetites, and no one ever said "I'm not hungry." Occasionally we would have ham and fried apples, a dish that I passed on to my own family (which they still relish).

Summers were short on rainfall, and pastures became stunted and dry. Rowena and I were delegated the job of herding the cows along the roadside. To the East of our place was the old riverbed with lots of trees and grass. While the cows munched away on the tall grass, we would swing on the grapevine swings, and make crowns for our heads, using small sticks run through cottonwood leaves to make a headband. What fun! When we herded West of the house, the riverbank was on the North side of the road. This was the high side of the river bank. While herding one day, the bull got too close to the edge of the bank and it caved off. He fell to the bottom. He was not injured, but we were really frightened, and ran home to tell Dad what had happened. By the time we got back, the bull had wandered over to the low side of the bank and walked up to join the rest of the herd.

One summer it was so hot and dry, the upland crops were withering and dying. There had been heavy rains West of us, and the river was running nearly bank full. There was a 36 inch metal tube that ran under the road to drain the water back into the river after it had flooded our land. There was a cap on the end to prevent the water from pouring out into our field. One evening after Dad had determined the water was no longer rising, he decided to open the cap and let the water flow into the fields to irrigate. We tied a rope around Dad's waist in case he should slip and fall into the water. Dad could not swim, due to a crippled arm received in an accident when he was a child. This irrigation project resulted in a bumper crop of corn and kaffer corn, a sorghum-like grain.

After a hard freeze, the corn would ripen, and it was time to harvest before heavy snows fell. Corn pickers, men with team and wagon, would hire out to pick. One side of the wagon was built up with bang boards (extended sideboards), so the ears of corn would fall into the wagon as the picker gave them a sling. Men were paid by the bushel, and a good picker could pick l00 bushels a day. Early mornings were quiet and the sound of the ears of corn hitting the bang boards could be heard for miles around.

Harvest Time

One of the daily chores was gathering the eggs. Nests were in the hen house, under the granary, in the hay loft, or any place a hen could hide her nest. Occasionally, we would find a soft shelled eggs. Then Mama would say it was time to give the hens some "grit." I would gather up pieces of broken dishes, lay a board across a metal stand, and with a hammer, crush the pieces into fine bits to feed the chickens. Later oyster shell was available, so this job was eliminated.

My father, being from a wooded area of Pennsylvania, planted lots of trees around the farmstead. He would go to the river, dig up a suitable tree and transplant it by the house. There were American Elm, Hackberry, Box Elder and Ash trees providing shade all around the house.

Each of us had our assigned chores. While Mama was preparing breakfast, Agnes would prepare lunches for all the kids attending school. I can still remember the line of syrup pails sitting in the kitchen waiting for the kids to leave for school. Blanche never cared for outside work, so it was her job to help Mama with the housework. Beth, Rowena and I inherited (by default) the farm chores such as gathering eggs, feeding livestock, milking cows, etc. By the time I was old enough to be of much help, Mabel, Gladys and Ruth had left home.

Some years later, Dad purchased a used radio, and evenings were spent listening to Amos and Andy, Fibber McGee and Molly, Jack Benny and other such entertaining programs. Maybe this is one of the reasons I enjoyed the 1980s television program "The Waltons," as it brought back memories of a large family in depression days. However, Olivia Walton had life far easier than my Mama did. Mama never had an electric iron; just the old flat irons with removable handles, heated on top of the cook stove.

The Old Radio

Downs was a bustling little town when I was a kid. The Railroad Roundhouse was located there, and this brought trade from a large area. There were two banks, two bakeries, two men's clothing stores, two variety (5 & 10 cent) stores, a hardware store, a paint and wallpaper store, three mercantile stores, a hotel, a farm implement store, a jewelry store, four grocery stores and a movie house. Cream and eggs were traded for sugar, flour and any other staples we needed. We usually had five gallons of cream each week, and this made for good trading.

During the Depression, butterfat got as low as 10 cents per pound, and eggs at 10 cents per dozen. Dad would take a can of cream to sell, and that money had to buy a bale of hay for the dairy cows. Many good dairy herds were sold due to lack of feed for the cattle.

Saturday night was movie night, and often a glass dish (usually a candy dish or fancy platter), was given away with each ticket sold. I remember the news reels well, and will never forget the night I saw "Gone With the Wind."

It Pays To Be "The Baby"

My parents had total authority over their children and none of the kids gave them any trouble. I can't remember Dad spanking me, but no doubt he did at least once; and once was usually enough. Mama scolded, but was usually too kind-hearted to give us the spankings we no doubt needed. All she needed to say was, "Wait until I tell your Dad." I doubt she ever told him, but the threat of it sure kept us in line. There was only one time I can remember of Mama really losing her temper.

One hot day the cattle had to be watered and the tank was dry, since there had been no wind for a few days to power the windmill. The cattle were driven a short distance down to the river to drink. It was no problem to get the cattle to the water, but getting them back to the corral was another story. Mama apparently had given instructions to we "three little kids" as we were called (Beth, Rowena and myself). While the cattle were drinking, we were playing in the car parked by the front yard gate. As the cattle came up from the river we were supposed to stand at designated places so they would go into the corral and not out into the field west of the house. Before we knew what was happening, the cattle were scattered all over the place instead of being in the corral. After Mama had them rounded up and had the gate closed, she came up to the car with a lilac switch in hand and proceeded to give Beth and Rowena several lashings. I don't know how I escaped punishment, but my two sisters felt I should have received the same as they did. The old expression "she's the baby" was used in my behalf when several such things happened at home.

Hobbies

Summer vacations were boring and long. I spent many hours leafing through the Sears Catalog. We called it our wish book, as all we could do was wish for things we would like to have but had no money to buy. One day, I came across a dressing table that really struck my fancy and decided I would try to make one for my bedroom. Dad had many carpenter tools and I was always watching him to see what each tool was used for. I went into the shop and searched around to find what I needed for this project. My sister, Blanche, asked what I was doing and when I told her, she sneeringly remarked, "You can't build a dressing table." Rowena added to her words of discouragement with, "What a joke. I'll bet you can't do it." This just strengthened my determination. I searched for materials to use and came upon two wood orange crates. I shouted, "Hurrah! These are exactly the same height, and the dividers can be used for shelves."

Woodworking Tools

I worked on this project in secret, all the while planning just how I could get this masterpiece put together. I gathered scraps of wood, hinges and nails, and a long board for the top. I also decided I needed a drawer in the center.

As the dressing table took shape, I realized I would have to cover the rough crates, and that a gathered fabric skirt around the whole thing would really dress it up. As the table was being finished, my sisters were still making fun of me and my creation. This caught the attention of my Dad and he came to the shop to see what the fuss was all about. Was he ever impressed with my handiwork! He was amazed that I had even built a sliding drawer in the center between the two crates. His approval of my project took the wind out of my sisters' sails, and it was no longer a joke.

This masterpiece more than deserved a piece of fabric to finish it off. Mother ordered the fabric for the table, and I could hardly wait until it arrived. With Mama's help, we gathered the fabric and fastened it to the sides and fixed an opening for the center by sliding it on the hinged 1" x 1"s. By using only materials available, I completed and used this table for several years, and it served its purpose. This was the beginning of a lifetime of "making do."

After completing my project, Blanche remarked, "Give Frances a hammer, a saw and a razor blade, and she can build anything."

High School

We girls attended and graduated from Downs High School in town. Going to high school from the country was a challenge. About half my freshman class were country kids. I liked all my teachers until my sophomore year, when we got a new superintendent named W. W. Bell. He only lasted a year. He was a poor teacher, had little control over his students, was overweight, and being kids, we made fun of him.

We had lots of fun and no doubt gave the teachers a few gray hairs. There were 42 kids who graduated in 1933, my senior year. The evening of our graduation, shortly after all parents and students had gathered in the auditorium, a high wind storm blew in and the power went out. We carried forth with the program using flashlights for some lighting. We students walked across the stage in the dark to receive our diplomas. We did not have caps and gowns, as no one had the money for such things.

My older sisters became teachers, and attended Hayes Teachers College through the summer months in preparation for the coming school term. My oldest sister, Mabel, taught for many years and earned a Life Certificate to teach in the Kansas school system. Agnes and Blanche were also teachers. Ruth was the only daughter to choose the nursing profession. After graduation, Beth went on to become an office clerk in Hutchinson, and Rowena and I were left at home. Gladys was the only one to marry right out of school; although in later years she worked in many different jobs.

.

Fran's parents, Frank and Hattie Carey (date unknown)

Fran's Family Homestead - Downs, Kansas

Fran's First Grade Class at
Prairie Bell School House
She's the one in the front
in the black dress.

Fran and Lucille
(date unknown)

Fran's high school graduation photograph
Downs, Kansas - June 1933

Floyd and Fran's wedding portraits - January 30, 1938

Floyd and Fran's first home, Portis, Kansas

Fran's baby lambs

Floyd and the "company car" - Hutchinson, KS (1947)

Mama Carey and her daughters (1953)
Front row, left to right: Mabel, Mama Hattie, Gladys
Back Row, left to right:
Agnes, Ruth, Rowena, Blanche, Rowena, Fran

Floyd's parents, Bert and Kate, Floyd, Linda and Fran
Osborne, Kansas (1948)

Hattie, Linda and Fran
Hutchinson, KS (1948)

Fran with Linda
Hutchinson, KS (1948)

Fran with Harriet and
Linda (1953)

Harriet and Linda
Family Farm House near
Osborne, KS (1953)

The Frazier Family's Easter trip to
Colorado Springs, CO (1958)

Floyd, Fran, Linda and Harriet
Denver, CO (June 1962)

Fran and Floyd portraits
Denver, Colorado (1964)

Gladys, Blanche, Beth, Rowena and Fran
Colorado Springs, CO (1964)

Fran and Floyd
Christmas 1965
Denver, CO

Fran, Floyd, Harriet and Linda
Christmas 1965 , Denver

Fran poked a lot of fun at Harriet for her love of the Beetle's music. One day in 1966, she decided to imitate Paul.
Denver, CO

Fran and Harriet,
(date unknown)
Colorado Springs, CO

Fran, Harriet and Carrie
(date unknown)
Denver, CO

Fran at Four Corners (Colorado,
Utah, Arizona, New Mexico), (1983)

Fran in the Redwoods
Forest, California
(1992)

Fran at Windsor Castle,
England, (August 1985)

Fran at Pebble Beach, CA
(June 1982)

Fran and Linda
Columbia, CA Jail, (June 1982)

Family reunion
Osborne, KS
Front row:
Gladys, Ruth, Blanche
Back Row:
Fran, Rowena
(1990)

Fran showing off her quilt
Chandler, AZ
(December 2005)

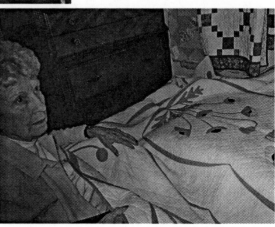

Fran, Harriet and Carrie
Christmas 1985, Denver, CO

Fran and Harriet Quilting
Christmas1985, Denver, CO

Fran's 80th Birthday
Chandler, AZ (1995)

Gladys' 90th Birthday
Colorado Springs, CO (1992)

Fran and Whitney
Arvada, CO (1993)

Fran with Whitney
and Sabrina,
Chandler, AZ
(1997)

Fran in her Phoenix back-
yard. Harriet gave her this
tree for her birthday.
Chandler, AZ, (1997)

, Carey Family Reunion, Osborne, Kansas (June 1990) There are 5 sisters in this photo: Blanche, Ruth, Rowena, Gladys and Fran. Four generations took part in this celebration.

Fran's portrait, (1978)

Fran's portrait, (1987)

Fran's portrait, (1992)

Fran and Linda,
(July 2005)

Fran's 90th birthday with quilt Harriet made for her
December 15, 2005

Jacob's Ladder

Chapter 7
The Great Depression

Times became harder in the l930s. Crops were shorter, rainfall became less and less, and the soil dryer and dryer. People had little or no money, as the rural areas depended on farming. If the farmers had no crops to sell, it affected everyone. Money was scarce as hen's teeth. Even though fabric was selling for ten cents a yard, it was not easy to come up with enough cash to purchase fabric for a quilt, so the scrap bag was a gold mine for quilters. We would trade pieces with neighbors and friends, or perhaps those who didn't piece quilts would donate their scraps to local clubs. The story is told by some that quilts were pieced from old garments. This was not the case in my time. By the time the garments were too worn to wear, they were torn into strips, sewn together and wound into balls for weaving rag rugs. Mama would send these to a weaver to be woven into strips to cover the floor in the winter.

In the late 1920s and early 30s, the national economy began to deteriorate. Banks went broke, people lost their life savings and everyone became poor. Many people were unemployed, and in cities, people formed what were called bread lines where food was donated to the poverty-stricken. Farmers were among the more fortunate, and even though farm prices had hit bottom, we always had enough to eat.

I graduated from high school in the Spring of 1933. The Great Depression was well under way and no one had any money. Continuing one's education was out of the question, except for a very few. Jobs for high school graduates were nonexistent, as family providers were jobless too. This left my sister Rowena and I to do odd jobs, such as living with families as their hired girl for a small wage. Fifty cents a day was about all one could expect, and we were glad to get that. I remained at home for a year or so after graduation. This was during the "black blizzard" days. Dust storms, as a result of the drought, plagued the farmers for several years. The soil was parched and dry. Many wells in the county failed, and water hauling became a daily duty. During these depressing days, Mama, Rowena and I pieced and quilted many quilts. This was a worthwhile pastime, and handwork of some sort helped to shorten the seemingly endless dark days created by dust in the air hiding the sun.

Blowing Dust

The "Dirty Thirties"

A dust storm was a harrowing experience, and unless one has lived through it, it is hard to believe. The day after a storm everyone was trying to clean their houses of this silt which seemed oily and hard to remove. One of our neighbor ladies was planning to have a party on a Sunday night. She came to Mama and asked if she could use one of us to help her clean. I went to her house and we swept, dusted and scrubbed to get this awful stuff cleaned up. I was cleaning, when her husband came into the room and said, "I know how so much dust gets into the house. It comes down the chimney and blows through the draftout." I guess that was supposed to be a joke, but there wasn't much humor in it to me. The newspapers stated the dust reached from the Dakotas' to Texas. Some areas were hit harder than others, due to spotty rainfall in parts of the state. Western Kansas was hit the hardest, as there was no growth on the land for miles around and the dust piled up along the fence rows so the wire fence was completely covered.

No one can imagine what the "dust bowl" days were like. My first experience happened on a Friday evening. Six of us kids started out to attend a dance in Downs. After picking up one of our group, and while we were driving down the street, this seemingly black curtain dropped before us, cutting our vision to zero. We inched our way to the dance hall, avoiding a collision. Everyone's faces were covered with dust. Two of the boys tried walking to the drug store to call our parents to let them know we were okay. The guys could tell where they were by feeling the building fronts, arriving at the drugstore only to find all telephone wires were down and they were unable to call anyone. Everyone stayed at the dance hall until it started to snow and clear the air so we could see our way home. What a mess! Oily silt covered everything. The silt was so fine no structure could keep it out. The next day, we took shovels and scooped the thickest dirt off the floors, then covered our faces with damp cloths and used brooms and mops to really clean. This was the first of many "black blizzards" to come, and we devised ways of coping with them. When we would see the black cloud coming from the Northwest, we would wet sheets and blankets and hang them over the windows and doors. This kept the air clean enough to breathe, although it meant lamplight in midday. During this time there was little to do except stay in the house out of the wind, which seemed to blow constantly.

Many years after this the attics still had silt in them. If any hammering was done inside, you would breathe this fine dust as it sifted into the room.

Doing chores in the evenings during these storms was a challenge. My sister Rowena and I would tie a rope around our waists and hold it so we wouldn't get lost. This seemed to go on endlessly.

Quilting as a Way to Pass Time

This was when we started piecing quilts in earnest. My father was an avid reader and he took a daily newspaper, The Kansas City Star. This was an important regional newspaper, reaching Missouri, Kansas, Arkansas and Oklahoma. Rural America was receiving a common newspaper, and from September 1928 through May 1931 it always printed quilt patterns for the ladies. This was something to look forward to, hoping there would be a new quilt pattern in the paper that was just the one we wanted to piece. Mama brought out the scrap bags, and we pressed the pieces, as mother decided which pattern we were going to use. There had to be enough of the same fabric for a block. Mama made templates from cardboard boxes and did all the cutting, as she was very particular about cutting on the grain. After the pieces were cut, the fun part started – laying out the squares and half squares to form a pattern. It didn't take long to get a top pieced, as there was nothing else to do with our time.

I don't know where pre-washing fabric came into the picture, as scraps were small, and no one in their right mind would wash and iron these pieces. Quilts were made a bit larger to allow for shrinkage. All cotton was the only fabric used for quilts. Cotton batting or wadding was used for filler. For summer weight quilts, a cotton sheet blanket was often used in place of batting, and required less quilting. This made a light weight quilt for use in warmer weather. Scraps left from home-made dresses were used for piecing, with no particular plan for color. Fabric varied from loosely woven to finer weave such as calico, gingham and "wash goods," as it was called. Dark colors were used for house dresses so as not to show the soil, since washing was a big job. In the late 20s and early 30s, the fabric industry had advanced to brighter colors, and was called print. This was colorful fabric with flowers and designs printed on the colored background. This was an exciting time for home sewers; no longer the dull drab colors for house dresses. Crazy patchwork quilts were made from scraps of wool left from clothing. Winters were cold, and wool skirts and dresses were winter attire. There was no pattern for this type of quilt, usually called comforters. They were tied, not quilted.

Silks, satins, velvets and brocades were used along with the wool pieces. Fancy stitches were embroidered along the seams. I have repaired a number of these quilts where the silks and brocades had disintegrated and had to be replaced with a comparable fabric. This was a challenge. Although a lot of work was involved, enjoyed it. I didn't show any interest in quilting until I was 11 or 12 years of age, when I tried my hand at this art. I would sew in a few stitches, Mama would examine them and say, "Frances, you could catch your toes in those stitches," so I ripped them out and tried again. Soon, Mama agreed that my stitches were okay for her quilts.

Summers were long and boring, so I decided I would try piecing a quilt. Mama did not waste her good scraps, so she gave me some sub-standard fabric, as she was certain I would cut up the pieces but never finish a quilt. To everyone's amazement, I hand pieced a Bear's Paw in blue and white. Mother regretted not giving me better fabric to work with but I finished it and we quilted it. Eureka! My first quilt!

We had a battery powered radio, so we stitched away while listening to programs of Amos & Andy, Fibber Magee & Molly, Jack Benny and other such programs that brought humor to our lives. I don't remember how many quilts we pieced, but after each top was completed, it went into the frame where endless stitching started. Our quilt frames consisted of 4 x 4s held together at the corners with C-clamps. This was laid over the backs of four kitchen chairs, rolled as we quilted. Late evening the frame was removed from the chair backs and leaned against the wall to be out of the way, as the room was quite small. Next morning after the morning chores were done, the quilt frame was placed back on the chairs and the stitching began.

Groups of ladies living in the same neighborhood would form a Club. Each Club had a name. The one my mother belonged to was the B-Ys Club. Each Club would put in a quilt and all the members would help. This was what was called a quilting bee.

Everyone got caught up in the "Sunbonnet Baby" quilt craze. I now have one that my sister never finished, and the one I made one for myself long ago has worn out. Next I made a "Japanese Fan" top and an appliquéd "Tulip" top, which I never got set together until years later.

There was a period of time after the dust storms, that quilting died out. I have thought about this in later years and I believe quilting was a stigma that brought back memories of that desperate period and, being poverty stricken.

The Grasshopper Invasion

The summer of 1935 saw a revival of life in the soil. Our first crop of wheat in what seemed years, was long overdue. I helped Dad run the wheat binder and shock the wheat. This was the summer of the grasshopper invasion. Large yellow grasshoppers flew in swarms, stripping the leaves from the trees. While riding the machinery, one would light on your back and eat holes in your shirt. Your first knowledge of their presence would be when they started chewing on your skin; then it was time for a hard slap to rid yourself of the pest. Hand tools such as pitch forks and hoe handles were jammed down into shocks of wheat to prevent the grasshoppers from roughing them up by chewing on them. Mid-afternoon would find the shady side of fence posts a bright yellow hue of grasshoppers. Trees were as bare as winter. Trying to save our first crop from the "hoppers," the County furnished the ingredients for poison bait. A mixture of wheat bran, molasses and arsenic was hand spread around fence rows and in pastures before daylight each morning. This was a daily chore for Dad and me. I drove the car, pulling a trailer with the bait loaded in tubs. As we moved along, Dad scattered the bait. Just as daybreak appeared, the hoppers would come out to feed on the bait and then they would hunt shade to die. Under wheat shocks and in shady places, one could scoop up dead hoppers by the bucket full.

Earning A Living

After helping Dad on the farm for a while, I lived-in with one family and cared for their little girl for $2.00 a week, while her parents operated a shoe store. In the fall of 1936, I worked in Luray, Kansas, for a family with two pre-school boys and a six week old baby for $4.00 per week. Caring for the baby and doing the laundry occupied most of my time. One day of washing and two days of ironing used up a goodly portion of the week. I was 30 miles from home and didn't have transportation to get home every weekend. However, my sister Blanche lived about eight miles out in the country, so I saw that part of my family quite often.

In November of 1937, my Father wrote me a card saying I could have the job of working for the Bates family. This was close to home, and known as one of the better places to work. Modern conveniences such as electricity, a furnace and indoor plumbing made working there a step up in the world. Carrie Bates Dillie had been a high school instructor of mine. I always admired her, even though I knew little of the rest of the family. I fit in with the family real well and it seemed like a second home, even though they were no longer living on the farm. My only granddaughter was named after this lady, whom both my daughters always admired.

Monkey Wrench

Chapter 8
Dating and Marriage

Being a country girl, it was not easy to get acquainted with boys other than those of surrounding neighborhoods. There were 47 kids in my freshman class when I entered high school in the fall of 1929. About half of the class were country kids and I had no interest in any of the boys. There was little social life except the movies and dances. One young man, Sam Warner, who was in the eighth grade, had his eye on me. He owned a Model T car and we would go out in groups. He was quite good looking and a good dancer. He taught me to dance on the sly, as my parents were against dances. I never could understand why, as they attended barn dances when they were young. Two of my uncles (Mama's brothers) played in the dance band; Uncle Bud played the violin, and Uncle Arnold played the French horn. Since we weren't supposed to go dancing, movies were about all the entertainment available.

Four boys (including Sam), stole a load of wheat and, of course, got caught and arrested. The other three boys parents bailed them out, but Sam, having no father, was sent to the reform school in Hutchinson, Kansas. Needless to say, that ended our courtship. I dated several young men from surrounding areas, but had no particular interest in any of them. I met Floyd Frazier at a card party. Not long after he asked me for a date, and I accepted. I really didn't care much for him at first, but I guess he just grew on me. Anyway we dated for four years, and once or twice a week he would come to my house.

After the drought and Depression, 1937 saw the first sign of a wheat crop. Floyd had spent the previous winter husking corn in Nebraska, and with the prospect of a wheat crop, he considered marriage. Floyd's dad owned a small four room house in Portis, Kansas. This little house was moved out on the ranch west of Portis and placed on a foundation. This was to become the first home of Mr. & Mrs. Floyd Frazier.

We were married on January 30, 1938, the coldest day of the year, at Minneapolis, Kansas by the Reverend Fred Blanding. Rev. Blanding had been pastor of our church in Downs, and was a good friend of my father's. My sister Beth and her husband accompanied us. Upon our return to the family home, a reception was served to a large group of relatives and friends.

We were too poor to consider a honeymoon, so we settled in our little cottage to begin building a life of our own. My wedding dress was a two-piece navy blue dress trimmed in navy and white stripe, and I wore black T-strap high heeled shoes. I had to have something practical to wear, as I could only afford one dress-up outfit.

Wedding gifts were few and inexpensive, as money was still very scarce. While I was working for a meager income, I managed to accumulate some items for my hope chest. This included a set of china, silver, linens, a complete set of Warever cookware, and, of course, my quilts. The quilts were used until threadbare, but the Warever is still my favorite cookware and has lasted 58 years.

Hard work was the way of life after marriage. We lived just across the creek from Floyd's folks, and for a year or so had little to call our own. I raised chickens, so we had our own eggs, and I helped with the milking of Floyd's dad's cows for milk and cream to use. Later, we converted the lower barn nearby to a milking barn and bought a few cows of our own. This gave us a little income from cream and eggs for groceries and other necessary items.

Before we were married, Floyd had a flock of sheep. Harold Coop was the Frazier's hired hand, and he and Floyd were always up to some devilment. One day Floyd told Harold to take a bucket of grain into the pen and feed the buck (male sheep). Harold did as instructed and after the buck had eaten a portion of the grain, Floyd told him to take it away. As Harold turned to go to the barn, the old buck took after him, and Harold had a real race to safety. Floyd knew this would happen and he nearly died laughing.

We continued raising sheep after we were married. When the ewes had twins, she would sometimes claim only one lamb and the other  was left an orphan. This happened several times and at one time I was feeding eight little lambs on the bottle. These little lambs followed me everywhere, and I felt like Mary and her little lamb. Soon they were turned out to pasture with the rest of the flock. I was always sad when it was time to take the lambs to market.[10]

A Baby Lamb

For the first few years of my marriage, clothes washing was done on a washboard. We had a small wash house with a small stove where water was heated in a galvanized boiler. After a while, Floyd acquired a gasoline powered washing machine for me. This was a giant step upward in laundry, and all my sisters were envious.

The War Years

In l939 the U.S. entered the war on the European front. All the young men were drafted and required to sigh up for duty. The boys who were farmers were deferred, as food production was a dire necessity. Food stamps were issued to all families. Food rationing was unheard of up until this time. Sugar was the hardest for farmers, as canning time required more sugar than we were allotted. Meat rationing was equally bad for city people, but farmers with their own meat would trade meat stamps for sugar stamps. Gasoline was rationed except to farmers. These were minor inconveniences compared to the hardships the European countries were suffering. In 1941, Japan attacked Pearl Harbor. War was now being waged on two fronts. These were heart breaking days, as a number of local boys were among the casualties. The lack of manpower in the factories brought women in for replacements. Women went into the plane factories, tire factories and any place where there was a manpower shortage. This was where women gained their independence, knowing they were capable of earning a salary; money

---

[10] Mama would never eat lamb, saying there was no way she could eat something when she was reminded of the babies she raised on the bottle.

they had never had before. After the war ended, many women continued at their factory jobs. Was this the beginning of Women's Lib?

At the end of the war, there were big celebrations in the cities and towns everywhere. People knew a bomb had been dropped on Japan. but never imagined what destruction, terror and death it brought on so many innocent human beings. We were happy the war was over and our boys would be coming home. One of the boys in my high school class died in the Battan Death March.

In l940 we had our first good wheat crop since the dust storms. The war was on so hired help was impossible to find. We had a self-propelled combine pulled by a Case tractor. I was riding in the grain bin to keep the grain leveled off – to keep from losing any of the precious grain while crossing ditches. We started cutting through a draw where the wheat was heavy, and the machine got clogged. Floyd called for me to come and get on the tractor. We pulled all the straw we possibly could get out of the machine, Then he told me to start the tractor. I didn't know what he planned to do, so I followed his instructions, put the tractor in gear and heard him scream. I looked around and saw his foot was caught. I shut off the gas and the tractor died, letting the combine stop so he could remove his foot, which was badly bruised and lacerated. He crawled under the combine for shade and I started running for the truck to get him to the doctor. Due to this accident we lost most of our crop, as all the neighbors were busy with their own harvest, and finding someone to work for us was impossible. Escal Booz, a long time friend of Floyd's, came out evenings after work and finished cutting our wheat.

After trying to farm with this injury, Floyd was told by the doctors he would have to stay off his foot or he would lose it. My brother-in-law was selling Bowes Seal Fast: tire repair products, a must during the war since new tires were still rationed. Floyd decided to try the selling game, and found it to his liking. He found he was a very good salesman. We decided to sell our livestock and machinery and start a new life. We moved to Hutchinson, Kansas, bought a little bungalow and lived there for several years. The Wade Patton Insurance Company was advertising for a Policy Writer for their office. My brother-in-law was a customer of theirs, and he persuaded me to apply for the job. He took me to their office and introduced me. In a few days I got a call saying I got the job. It was my first office job, and I was delighted.

Visiting New York City

In December of 1945, our friend Escal Booz was in the Navy, and we received word that he was in the hospital, dying of cancer. Floyd wanted to see Escal once again, so we pooled our meager savings and headed for Brooklyn, New York. We arrived at Grand Central Station on a gloomy, snowy morning after riding many hours on the train. Sailors and soldiers were everywhere. Escal's mother had accompanied us and she planned to stay at the hospital. Escal had rented a room with kitchen privileges, and we stayed there during this time. What an experience – so many people in one place. Children were using spoons to play in the dirt in a four foot square area with one tree growing in the center; a real life example of the book *A Tree Grows in Brooklyn*. Open markets, including fish markets, lined the sidewalks and were not for the weak-stomached.

We took several bus trips to see some of the city, such as Rockefeller Center, Times Square, and the RCA Radio City Music Hall. Edward R. Murrow was broadcasting the news. Television was in its infancy and we saw some of the first. The sets provided viewing from a 4 x 6 inch screen. After a week in New York, we returned home. We had a two hour layover in Chicago. With that much time, why not do a little sightseeing? We stepped out of the train station into the worst frigid air I had ever felt. Those were the days when ladies wore dresses and nylons; the era before ladies in trousers became fashionable. That bitter cold wind told us Chicago was no place for us.

Dad and "The Boys"

Dad had eight sons-in-law. He accepted them all and they got along well. At holiday time when they were all together, they would play cards. However, playing for money was forbidden in our household. When a few or all of us got together, Dad would often join the guys in the wash house for a drink of whiskey. He was not against one or two, but the guys knew when enough was enough.

Gladys, my second oldest sister, was the first to marry and leave home. She became Mrs. Lloyd Hettinger in a ceremony that took place at our home. A makeshift alter was placed in the corner of the living room, and this is where the bride and groom stood. Mabel and Joe Otte were their attendants. I was the ring bearer, and I remember so vividly carrying the ring. It had been placed in the center of a white aster, and I had to carry the flower by the stem. I squeezed the stem so tightly I don't know how I managed to keep it erect. I still have the little white batiste dress I wore at the wedding.

Lloyd was a salesman who sold Baker Products house to house. Later, after they were married, he started selling nursery stock such as fruit, shade and ornamental trees. They moved around a lot, finally settling in Belleville, Kansas. They bought a house and lived there for a number of years. While I was still a little girl, I went to their house one time to spend a week. Gladys wanted me to look like other kids my age, so she cut off my braids and I had short hair for the first time. She also let me wear knee socks. When Mama and Dad came after me, Mama was outraged. She though Gladys was leading me down the path of sin.

Mabel married Eugene Kurtz from Alton, Kansas, whom she had met while teaching in that area. Agnes met and married Jim Stuart from Smith Center. Ruth met Milo Johnson while working as a nurse in Belleville, and Blanche met John Applegate while working as a PBX operator in the Cheyenne District near Luray, Kansas. Beth married Clifton Eisiminger in Hutchinson, and Rowena married Delose Rouse, who hailed from the Downs area.

The Loss Of The Farm

During the Depression years, the bank foreclosed on the mortgage it held on Dad's land. My folks were permitted to remain on the farm as long as they were able to keep up with that sort of work. It was difficult for the folks, as all the girls were gone by then and were pursuing their own lives. In 1939, my parents sold all unnecessary articles, along with the farm equipment. They moved into Downs, where Dad had purchased a neat little house and modernized it. Here was home to them until the time of my Father's death.

The Train Accident

In 1944, my father was killed in a train/auto accident. He and Mama were on their way to the train station to pick up Uncle Arnold and Aunt Stella. Dad took one of the back roads in Downs, where the railroad crossing ran through the stockyards. On this particular Sunday morning, the train men had unloaded a car of cattle and bumped the empty car to send it down the tracks. There was no flagman to warn of the "flying switch" and as Dad started across the tracks, this empty boxcar hit his car, crushing it and killing my father. We always thought he died of a heart attack, since there were no severe bruises on his body. Mama was riding in the back seat of the car. As she was trying to crawl out of the broken back window, two men driving by stopped and helped her out, and took her home. She had some back injuries, but other than that she was not badly injured.

Mama tried living alone, but could not cope with the loneliness after so many years of having some of the family with her. She sold the house and furnishings, and took turns living in her girls' homes, spending more time with Gladys and me than the others. She spent her last few years in Springfield, Missouri, where Gladys cared for her until her death in 1953.

Mother was living with me in 1947. She had pieced quilts for all her grandchildren, but with nothing to do, she cut diamond shapes from newspaper and used the smallest pieces of fabrics she could work with to make the points of a six point string star quilt. She had all the diamonds pieced, and took them with her to visit one of my sisters. My sister wanted to help her put the pieces together, not realizing there was a certain way that had to fit. When mother tried to set the corner blocks in, nothing fit, and she became discouraged. She returned to my home, and one day I came home from work, and found all these stars in the trash basket. I retrieved them, and vowed her thousands of stitches would not be wasted; that one day I would rip them up and set them together correctly. Mother didn't live to see this task completed, but I finished the piecing and quilted it. This was for my daughter Harriet; a quilt her Grandmother had pieced.

Chapter 9
Having A Family

When Floyd and I moved to Hutchinson, we both had to work to make ends meet. Due to lack of finances, we had to put off having a family. Finally, when I was 33 years old and had nearly given up ever having children, I discovered I was pregnant. We were both delighted. Floyd said he wanted a little girl and would name her Suzie. The name Linda Sue was chosen. Mother was living with me in Hutchinson when Linda was born on February 22, 1948. Mama was in second heaven to have a baby in her arms again. I let her hold and rock the baby as much as she wished.

I took maternity leave from my job at Wade Patton & Company, and returned to work when Linda was eight weeks old. Had Mother not lived with us at that time, I would have never left my child with anyone else. Linda was a good baby, and Mother enjoyed caring for her while I was working.

In the summer of 1950, the war was over and new tires were available, so patching the old ones was no longer necessary. The Bowes Seal Fast sales dwindled. Floyd met a man who had a farm near Sylvia, Kansas. Bill raised sheep, and he was looking for someone to take over the farming. Just after harvest we moved out to this farm, where Floyd took over the farming duties. He prepared the land for wheat planting. I don't remember exactly what happened, but there was a disagreement due to Bill not telling Floyd his ex-mother-in-law owned the land and was not agreeable to the deal Bill and Floyd had made. We saw there was trouble in the family, and decided this was no place for us. During this time, Floyd's father had a severe heart attack and his mother wanted us closer to them. She owned a farm East of Osborne, Kansas, and was dissatisfied with her tenant, so she rented the farm to Floyd, and we moved back to Osborne County.

Back to the Farm

When we returned to Osborne County, Mother stayed with us for some time. The farm house had no inside plumbing and poor heating. We had no indoor plumbing on the farm, so bathing was done in a galvanized bath tub placed in the kitchen near the heating stove. Water was heated on the cook stove and then poured into the tub. Living conditions were not good for her, so she went to live with Gladys in Springfield, Missouri, where she remained until her death.

Floyd saw that farming a small acreage was not making him a decent living He saw the need for a dairy in this area, as several farmers were milking cows and just selling the cream. He went to work organizing a Grade A Dairy Association.

In the Spring of 1952, we were in the early stages of building a Grade A dairy. We put up a metal storage building for wheat and hay. After that we converted the grainery to a milk house, with electric milkers and cooling tank. Every other day the milk hauler would pick up the milk, and along with others, haul it to Russell, Kansas for processing. This became the Osborne County Dairyman's Association.

In the meantime, I was pregnant with my second child. I was delighted to have another child, but in the back of my mind I wondered how I could manage two children and the work involved with the dairy. Plus, I had all the other jobs required of a housewife and mother to think about as well.

My second child, Harriet, was born on October 2, 1952. By the spring of 1953, the dairy set-up was completed. We were now a full fledged Grade A dairy, which demanded a good part of the forenoon cleaning. I bundled Harriet up, placed her in the baby buggy and took her with me. The barn was heated, and she was quite content while I was busy cleaning. Our dairy herd had increased to 40 registered cows, which meant keeping records on each one; one more job for me.

Buying feed and hay was an endless job, and we contracted a trucker to keep us supplied with hay and feed. His name was Vic Tobler, and he was as dependable as clock work. Hank Baldwin was the milk hauler, and quite often these fellows would join us for breakfast.

Music in The House

Blanche and John bought a farm close to the town of Luray, Kansas in 1951. The owner of the place had left an old Sears & Roebuck pump organ in the house, with the promise that he would move it soon. When Blanche and John moved into the house, the organ was still there. I had a fascination for this old piece of furniture, and told John if he ever wanted to get rid of it, I would like to have it.

The organ was moved out into the garage, where it remained for a period of time. John needed the room for a new pick up truck, and called the owner of the organ and told him he wanted it moved right away. John was told to give the organ to someone who would give it a good home. I received a call from Blanche saying if I still wanted that organ, I should come and pick it up.

The pump organ that Mama brought home.

That afternoon I took the truck and brought it home. It was full of mice nests and dirt. It took several days to get the thing looking good enough to be moved from the porch into the house. After many hours of scrubbing caked-on dirt, I got down to the wood, to discover it was solid walnut. After all the cleaning and replacing the bellows straps, it played as good as new. Both my daughters started music lessons on it, and it has been in my home ever since. It is now more of a conversation piece than a musical instrument.[11]

---

[11] That organ is still in the family. We moved it many times, and no matter where we were, it resided in our living room. It was quite the conversation piece. Upon Mom's passing, the organ made another move – this time to my niece's home in Laramie, Wyoming.

Family Life

My children had little entertainment. They had dolls and toys like most kids, but no place to call their own. From scraps of lumber left over from the new barn, Floyd built them a nice playhouse in the back yard. I built some kid-sized furniture for it and they now had a place they could call their own.[12]

I believed children should be read to, so I took time to read to them every night and to teach them to read. To this day, they are both avid readers. When Linda started first grade, we were still on the farm, and I had to drive 5 miles into town twice daily to get her to school. First grade was easy for her, but when she reached second grade, things got a bit difficult. Because I had taught her to read and write, and because she had learned how to write cursive, not just printing, her second grade teacher got mad. She wanted Linda to print and Linda refused. That began the challenges Linda had throughout her years of schooling.

Every Sunday morning after the chores were done, I'd dress the girls up in their Sunday best and the four of us were off to town for Sunday School and Church. It didn't matter the weather, or how tired we were, we seldom missed a Sunday.

The holidays were hard, as it was the same old grind with little time to do the extras. Dairy cows need to be milked twice daily and they don't care if it's a holiday. At Christmas time, my girls had new toys, even though they were few. Walking dolls were the "in" thing, and Linda had seen one in the store dressed as a bride. Like all little girls, she wanted one for Christmas. We bought each girl a walking doll, and

[12] My Mother never missed an opportunity to have a bit of fun. While Dad was the prankster, Mom was the one who found pleasure out of the smallest of events. When Harriet and I were small, and at the first good snowfall, Mom would get out the big scoop shovel and we would take turns riding in our very own sled. As we got older, we had sleds in various shapes and sizes. After we moved to Denver, and until Dad got sick, every year we would go sledding and tubing in the Rocky Mountain foothills. Dad enjoying the rides every bit as much as his "girls."

from my sewing supplies, I found a piece of ivory satin. I made the brides dresses and fashioned a full length veil and train from some old lace curtains. The girls were delighted and thought these were as good as the ones in the stores.

On Christmas Eve, Floyd would always take the girls for a walk to the dairy barn for some made-up reason. On the way back to the house, he would point up to the sky and say he'd just seen Santa take off from the roof and he was moving very fast. By the time they got back to the house, we had two very excited little girls. The age difference between Linda and Harriet became a challenge when Linda was 8 years old. She woke one night and saw me wrapping Christmas presents, and also saw where I hid them before Christmas Eve, when Santa Claus supposedly delivered them. This was proof to her that there was no Santa Claus and she told Harriet. Of course, Harriet came to me in tears, and it took some fast talking to calm a very upset little girl.

We never missed spending the holidays with my family. Sisters, husbands, and children would gather at one another's homes for the usual holiday feast. At Christmas we exchanged gifts by drawing names. We also never missed attending Sunday School and Church, and the girls were always in the Church programs.

I don't know how I found the time, but I made all the clothes for the girls, including their coats. These were made from donations of old coats from my sisters. I would rip up the old coats, turn the fabric wrong side out, and it was like new. I loved sewing for my girls, and Linda remembers feeling like she was the best dressed girl in school. [13]

[13] Along with the things she mentions above, Mom was a great cook and holiday time was where her true talents came out. She specialized in candy making and we made peanut brittle, fudge, divinity, caramels – you name it, we made it. Some recipes were one-time only; others were expected every year. Home made fudge and divinity (not the marshmallow kind) is a dying art and one that I'm proud to say I've inherited. At the end of this book, are Mama's recipes for fudge and divinity.

The Dairy Farm

Below are three photos that were part of a story published in the *Kansas Farmer,* November 6, 1954 edition. The title of the front page story was, "I Chose Dairying," and the subtitle was, "Floyd Frazier gathered ideas, remodeled buildings, added modern equipment, finds success....." The captions read just as they were printed.

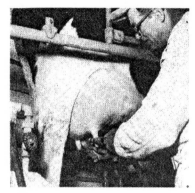

"Hot and cold water within reach, plus elevated stalls, making preparing cows for milking an easy job for Floyd Frazier, Osborne County dairyman."

"Mrs. Floyd Frazier can handle milk cans with this vacuum hoist. Here she is shown in milk room with daughters Linda Sue, right, and Harriet Jane. "

"Feed for cows is fed by gravity in the Frazier milking parlor, and milk is carried from cow to cans in milk room thru glass pipes."

Salem

Chapter 10
Moving To The City

In 1954, the Government started building a dam on the South Solomon River. This was to become Webster Lake; a lake created to hold the run-off from heavy rains. This body of water was to be used for irrigation and recreation. In 1957, our water supply began to fail and, needless to say, it is impossible to run a dairy without ample water. Floyd hauled water to aid the dwindling supply, but this could not continue. We made the decision to sell out. Preparation for the sale began, and it was held on February 25, 1958 – a great sale.

That night a violent winter storm blew in from the north. Heavy snow and strong winds blocked all the roads. We needed to get Linda to school in town, so. Floyd managed to get the truck through fields to get to Osborne. He arranged to rent an apartment from our attorney friend. That afternoon we packed all necessary items of food and clothing and moved to town. We remained there until the roads were cleared and we were able to get back home. It was quite an adventure for the girls, but quite a shock for Floyd and me. There were no cows to milk, and we were unable to get settled in Salina where we had purchased a house. There was nothing to do but wait for the snow to melt. We were so lucky though. Had we not sold out the day that we did, we would have lost everything. Many farmers lost cattle and other livestock in the blizzard that year.

With the proceeds of the farm sale, we purchased a new home in Salina, Kansas. This was the nicest home we'd ever lived in, and Floyd hired a professional decorator to furnish the place for us. We had indoor plumbing, which was such a luxury, and we had our very first television.

For Easter in 1958, we took our first family vacation. After we sold the farm, Floyd bought a new Pontiac, our first new car. It was real classy, and in my favorite color, lavender, which was popular that year. We drove to Hastings, Nebraska, the nearest "city" that had nice stores. Floyd bought us all a new set of clothes for our Easter trip, and I wore that suit for many years after. We drove to Colorado Springs, Colorado to visit my sister Beth and brother-in-law, Cliff. They didn't have room for us to stay with them, but Beth was the executive secretary to the president of the Interstate Gas Company. The company had access to a suite of rooms at the Antlers Hotel in downtown Colorado Springs. In 1958, the Antlers rivaled the Broadmoor Hotel for old world elegance and my girls felt like Cinderella – in new clothes, riding in a new car and staying in such an elegant place.

When we moved to Salina, Linda started at a new school in the fifth grade and Harriet was in the first grade. I was in second heaven in my new home, and was now settled in. It didn't take long to get restless, and I became active as a Brownie Scout leader. Floyd took a job selling boats. Boating was very popular, since there were several man-made lakes in the area. This did not prove successful, so he took a job as salesman for a farm implement company. Girl scouting did not keep me occupied enough, and I felt a need to go back to work. I applied for and was hired as secretary for the Alumni Association at Kansas Wesleyan College. The economy worsened, and lay-offs began. Floyd was last hired and first to be relieved of his job.

On the Move Again

In late 1959, he headed for Denver in search of employment. Jobs were available and once again it was moving time. In January 1960 we left Kansas for Colorado. We sold our house in Salina and purchased one in North Denver. This move was another one for the record books. It was the end of January, when the weather was very unpredictable. When the moving company left Salina with everything we owned, they told us they would meet us in Denver in three days. We packed kids and clothes in the car and took off. Floyd was not one for stopping, and decided to drive straight through – even though it was a seven hour drive and we didn't leave until close to 4 PM. We would go to Colorado Springs, where Beth had the suite at the Antle's Hotel reserved for us. We would go to Denver daily and do what we could in the house until our belongings got there. Little did we know that there was a severe storm following us all the way through.

We made it, but the moving van got caught in road closures. It was eight days before our furniture arrived! By that time, we were getting very tired of driving from Colorado Springs to Denver and back every day. It wasn't like it is now, no one had cell phones and all the phone lines were down; plus we did not have a phone in the new house. We had nothing to cook on, with, or eat off of, so we got our first taste of MacDonald's. It was a novelty at first, but after the fourth day of MacDonald's for lunch, it was getting real old. Finally, our van arrived and we could begin to feel like we were home.

Floyd went to work for Elcen Metal Company in a southern suburb, Englewood. I found a job as a scheduler for the Gates Rubber Company. Gates was on the way to Elcen, so Floyd and I carpooled every day. Gates Rubber Company was the largest manufacturing plant in Denver and they made rubber tires, hoses and belts. They were very good to their employees, and even had a gas station at the plant where employees could buy gas for their cars. If I remember right, the average cost for a gallon of gas was $0.23. And, because Gates subsidized the gas for employees, when we purchased gas from the company station, we received stamps. I saved those stamps every year, and redeemed them for cash in early December. This money was what we used to purchase our Christmas gifts. I continued working for Gates Rubber Company until my retirement in 1978.

In 1963, Floyd suffered a heart attack. His doctor put him on disability, and he was a broken man. He had been a robust hard worker all his life and now could do very little. He went through open heart surgery, gradually lost his will to live, and just gave up. His heart gave out, and he died on September 14, 1969, missing his 54th birthday by ten days.[14]

---

[14] I don't know what would have happened to our family if Mom hadn't been employed by Gates Rubber Co. It was her job got us through the rest. Mama never complained, but she must have been exhausted.

Life as a Widow

Right before Floyd died, he sold our house and bought us a nice new mobile home. His reason for this move was that he thought I could better care for a mobile home than the three bedroom ranch house we had. I was not consulted, and was not happy with that decision from day one. I never liked living in a mobile home, and although I made the best of it, when I finally got out of it and into a condo, I was a very happy person.

Linda graduated from high school in 1966 and went immediately into the work force. She married in March 1967 and divorced in March 1970. She held many jobs, each one being a step up for her. After her father died, I wanted her to go to college and get a degree, but she had never liked school and chose not to return to the classroom. Linda was always my independent, go-it-alone daughter, who made up her mind that the traditional life of husband and kids was not for her. Floyd did not like his new son-in-law, and I do believe he was a happy man right before he passed away, because he had gone with Linda to the attorney's office to file for divorce. I don't know how he would feel about Linda's gypsy way of life, but she has never looked back and appears to have no regrets.

Harriet was still at home and a senior in high school when Floyd died. She continued her education and graduated from Colorado State University in 1974 with a degree in clothing design and construction.

While Harriet was in college, Linda and I began to travel together. We made several trips to the desert Southwest, seeing most of Utah, Arizona, New Mexico and Colorado. We had a lot of fun on those road trips and did a lot of crazy things together.[15]

---

[15] Mama and I took a lot of chances on these trips. We'd get off on a country road, get lost, and never think twice about exploring further. We were never in an accident, nor did we end up spending the night in the car, although I think she often thought we were near disaster. We would pick up rocks, wild flowers, shells, whatever caught her interest that day. I still have two pieces of marbled granite that she picked up in Utah; they have moved all over the country with me and to this day I use them as doorstops.

Linda liked photography and while she took pictures of our travels, I kept journals of all the things we did and saw. I think she still has these scrapbooks of the trips we took.

In 1982, Mount St. Helens erupted in Washington state. Linda and I had tickets to fly to San Francisco. After the eruption, we weren't sure we would be able to make the trip, but the travel industry bounced back, the air cleared, and off we went, from May 25 to May 30. This was my first time in a commercial airplane and a great treat. This was also the first time we did not have a car at our disposal. We stayed in a hotel on Union Square and took bus tours all over the area. In six days there wasn't much we had not seen. One of our bus tours dropped us off at Fisherman's Wharf, giving us the option of taking the bus back to Union Square or finding our own way back. I said I'd like to walk and Linda was a good sport. Although we had ridden up and down the hills in both buses and on the cable cars, little did we know that our knees and feet were not up to the task. By the time we reached the hotel several hours later, all either of us could think of was getting our shoes off and putting our very sore feet to soak.

I'm a Grandma!

On June 7, 1974, Harriet married Richard Hargrave. In June 1976, a baby girl arrived, named Caroline Frances Hargrave. Harriet was a full time mother for three years. Becoming bored with housewife duties, she took machine arts classes, and became a roving teacher in adult education classes. She had an interest in quilting and made a quilt for a friend as a wedding gift. She found hand quilting a task too time-consuming – there had to be a better way. She began practicing quilting by machine, using the same method she had been teaching for machine embroidery. She pieced and quilted her first quilt by machine.

Harriet was planning to attend a seminar in Chicago on Mary Ellen Hopkins new method of piecing by machine. She had no original pattern for a pieced quilt so what to do? I suggested she take the quilt she had quilted by machine, since it was an original creation, but she didn't think it was a good idea. I folded the quilt up and placed it in her suitcase. When the time came for 'show and tell' in Chicago, her quilt was voted best of the show. Marti Mitchell, who was the organizer of the seminar, requested that she write a book on the art of machine quilting, which she did. That book, after several revisions, is still in print today.

In 1977, when Carrie was just a baby, Harriet and I decided we wanted to go on a trip back East. We rented a travel trailer, put it behind her car and off we went – Grandma, mother, and baby daughter. It must have been quite a sight to behold: two crazy women living for two weeks out of this little bitty travel trailer, while trying to keep a fussy baby happy. We had some great times on that trip, but there were times when we got very tired of each other's company. We traced my parents' journeys as best we could, visiting Hannibal, Missouri where my Mother hailed from; then on to Waynesburg, Pennsylvania where Dad had been born. We went back further, to the shores of Massachusetts, where we visited the graves of ancestors who had migrated from Bristol, England.

In 1985, Linda had an opportunity to relocate to Los Angeles. It almost broke my heart to lose my companion, but we all must cut the apron strings at some point,and she was well past due. She surprised me by inviting me to go to England with her in August, right before she moved. She packed up everything, sold her place, got our passports and off we went across the water. I had always been interested in tracing my family history and even more so after the trip back East with Harriet a few years before.

A Trip I'll Never Forget

We flew all night and arrived at Gatwick Airport outside of London about 10:00 AM Linda slept well on the flight over, but I had been restless, and all I wanted to do was to take a nap in a real bed. That was not to be. After collecting our luggage, we took the train from Gatwick into Victoria Station and caught a taxi to our hotel. Check in time at the hotel was not until 2:00 PM, but they did let us leave our luggage. After getting something to eat, we hopped on a double-decker bus for a tour of London. I was so sleepy I could hardly keep my eyes open, but Linda took it all in and made notes of where we had to return to explore further. We visited all of the tourist attractions on guided tours and also spent time walking the streets of London. After two days in London, we took the train back to Gatwick where we rented a car.

Linda has never been one to make reservations for anything, although she had reserved a car and the first two nights lodging in London. From then on, we were, in her words, winging it. When we arrived at the car rental place, they tried to give us a stick shift car. Linda said she could master driving on the wrong side of the road, but there was no way she could do both – drive a stick and do it all backward. The only automatic transmission they had left was a new black Mercedes that had a whopping six miles on it. I had never before, nor have I since, ridden in such a nice automobile. We practiced driving on the wrong side of the road that evening before heading for the country side the next day. Linda took to driving this way as if she'd been doing it all her life.

For the next five days, there were not many back country roads that we missed in the southern half of England. In Devon, I fell in love with Clotted Cream Caramels. In Brighton, we ate fish and chips. In Stratford-on-Avon we tried scones with clotted cream and jam. The dollar was strong that year, and we bought stuff like it was going out of style. Each of us had a matching set of luggage where the mid-sized piece fit in the large piece. We traveled over with one piece inside the other. Coming back, we had a total of four large bags that were packed to the gills, plus a bunch of carry on items as well. This was the trip of a lifetime for me!

Linda made sure we visited my ancestral home, Castle Cary. The castle had crumbled several hundred years past, and only the foundation remained of the manor house. We toured the graveyards and talked to the locals. We also visited Bristol, the shipping port that my ancestors sailed from to reach the New World.

We flew back to Denver, arriving home Monday evening. On Tuesday morning, we packed the car and headed for Los Angeles. I was beginning to wonder what time zone I was in. I helped Linda get settled in her apartment, then flew back home. I thought my heart would break when I boarded the plane in Burbank and she was standing outside waving goodbye.

This was the beginning of many plane trips for me. I would fly to wherever Linda had landed, and she and I would take short sightseeing trips together. Because of my gypsy daughter, I got to see a lot of this country, and I will always be grateful to her for the opportunity.

Chapter 11
Harriet's Treadle Arts

In the meantime, Harriet conceived the idea of opening a machine arts store. I agreed to help her get started. Opening date was April 10, 1981, and Harriet's Treadle Arts was now off and running. We taught classes, and little by little items for sale were added, including fabric. Now strip piecing quilting was in vogue, and Mary Ellen Hopkins' method was taught. The classes grew and the store expanded. I worked in the store whenever Harriet needed me, until she began traveling the circuit to teach her quilting methods – then I became a full time employee. [16]

We moved from the little house that was our original store to a larger location that we quickly outgrew. Things were going so well by now that we decided to purchase our own building, and Harriet's Treadle Arts still resides in Wheat Ridge, Colorado. In the meantime, Harriet was traveling more and more. Her marriage had broken up and I took on my third career. I was not only caregiver and surrogate Mom to my granddaughter Carrie, I was a store manager. I was still living in North Denver, now in the mobile home. I would pack my bag on Monday morning and head for Wheat Ridge. Harriet would be traveling, I would stay in her house taking care of Carrie and running the store, until it was time to go home on Friday evening or Saturday afternoon, depending on when Harriet returned home. This lasted for several years.

I finally got tired of making that drive and living out of a bag, so I sold the mobile home and bought a condo not far from Harriet's house. This made life so much better for all of us, as Carrie could stay with

---

[16] I don't have photos of any of the stores Mom and Harriet had. I can attest that each one was bigger and better than the last. They spared no expense to carry only the best quality merchandise and fabrics. Harriet would eventually go on to design her own line of fabrics and write several more books. Today, my sister is known world-wide for her knowledge and expertise in the art of quilting.

me every now and then, and if Harriet were home, I wasn't in the way. We had some great times, though, and for Mother's Day 1986, Harriet took me to Boston with her. She had a teaching job, but we sure got to see a lot of the area.

Our little quilt store grew to become the best quilt shop in the region. We became distributors for the Bernina sewing machine line, a company headquartered in Switzerland. As one of Bernina's top distributors in 1990, we qualified for a trip for two to their headquarters in Switzerland. Harriet and I flew to Zurich with a group and what a time we had. We toured the factory and I learned so much about sewing machines my head was swimming. But it wasn't all work; there were marvelous tours and it was so much fun.

We qualified again in 1992. This time Harriet was unable to go, but wanted me to take one of our employees. I was not sure about this but with the encouragement of Linda, Harriet and Carrie, Phyllis and I took off for a few days in Amsterdam. What a delightful trip. Once again we were with a group of Bernina people, and we got to tour the tulip fields, see the windmills and learn a lot about Holland and its people.

I have both of my daughters to thank for the many parts of this country and the world that I have had the chance to see. None of my sisters ever had the chances I have had, and my Mother and Dad would have been amazed at what I've done in my lifetime. Although I've had to work hard all my life, I've been given the gift of an adventurous family that has let me tag along.

One More Retirement

When Linda left the San Francisco area and decided to settle in Phoenix, I breathed a sigh of relief. She had been through an earthquake in Los Angeles in 1987 and had survived the big one in San Francisco in 1989. Although it didn't seem to bother her, I never knew what to expect next. After she had gotten settled in her apartment in Phoenix, she invited me to spend the winter of 1993 with her. She flew to Denver and drove my car down. I brought Whitney, my little poodle, and we learned to navigate around the Chandler area while Linda was at work. I found it amazing that I could grow a garden in the winter and that you really didn't have to wear a coat for most of the year.

We talked about my spending the winters with her in Phoenix and returning to Denver during the summer. I wanted to think about it, but after I got back to Denver in April, there was one of our usual spring blizzards. It suddenly occurred to me that I really didn't want to shovel any more snow; that I was getting entirely too old to put up with all the cold and inconvenience of winter. I called Linda and told her to start looking for a house, and that started my next adventure. We decided to build a brand new house which would be ready in early November 1994. By Memorial Day, 1994, I had sold my condo, packed my belongings, put it all in storage and was living in Phoenix. We had a two bedroom apartment with a cat and a dog. We moved into our new home on November 7, 1994. I told Linda that this was the nicest place I had ever lived, and that I wanted to die in my own bed in my new home.

I have enjoyed this home more than I thought possible. I have a garden that I can dabble in most of the year, and even have a couple of citrus trees that bear good fruit. Linda threw a party for me on my 80th birthday. She drives me to Denver every summer, and I spend a couple of months with Harriet and Carrie. Then Linda comes to get me before the cold sets in.

Some Final Thoughts

There was a period of time between marriage and family and retirement that I had no time for quilting. After I retired from Gates in 1978, I picked up where I had left off with quilting. I finished piecing, and quilted the tops I had made years before. I began teaching hand quilting at the store, and continued teaching until I retired from the store in 1994. I am now returning to my favorite pastime - quilting. I have a number of tops pieced just waiting for me to start my stitching.

Yes, many changes have taken place in these past 82 years.[17] Horse power gave way to tractors for farming and automobiles for transportation. Steam engines were replaced by diesel trucks for hauling freight, and air travel is now as common as the automobile for long trips. Televisions are a source of entertainment in nearly every home, and to watch the moon landing was something to be remembered.

I am very blessed and have lived a good life. Yes, there were hardships, but I was always able to make the best of a given situation. I had a good husband, and have two daughters and a granddaughter who care for me. I am secure in knowing that I will be cared for until the very end.

I look back and wonder if future generations will experience as many changes as have occurred in the 20th century. I'm glad to have lived to see all these changes and have, to the best of my ability, recorded them as they affected my life.

---

[17] Mama was 82 when she stopped writing. A few years later I tried to revive her interest in updating her manuscript, but she just wasn't up to the task.

Chapter 12
The Final Chapter

When I was working with Mama on this manuscript, I had no idea what I would do with it. I just knew that I wanted this piece of history in writing, because there would come a time I would no longer be able to ask her about her life. I have published three books thus far, and now that she is no longer with me, it only makes sense that this becomes the fourth.

Mama made her last summer trip to Denver in 2001, no longer able to navigate the stairs in my sister's home. Her last trip of any kind was back to Kansas in 2002 for the funeral of Blanche, the last sister to pass. I helped her travel that journey and it was not only a very emotional journey but a very tiring and rough one on her physically as well. By this time she was walking with a walker, she was no longer able to do much in her beloved garden, and the slowing down process had begun.

I had left the corporate world to work for myself in 1998. My first and second books were a result of her sharing her journey with me. I am an elder care consultant and my 13 years of hands-on experience with Mom earned me the equivalent of a college degree. If it were not for her and the experiences we had together, I would not be an author nor a professional speaker on the subject of aging and eldercare.

It's not often an adult daughter can, after many years of independence, successfully begin to share a home again with an aging Mother. The positive experience we had is a tribute to her willingness to accept me as an adult, no longer her child. We were mother and daughter yes, but first and foremost, we were friends.

During the last six months of her life, I did not feel comfortable leaving her alone. We hired non-medical home care, our Visiting Angels, to act as companions for her while I was out earning a living. I moved my office into the guest room and she seemed more at ease when I was there.

I planned a celebration for her 90th birthday on December 15, 2005. My sister and niece flew in as a surprise, and she was truly queen for a day. We had caregivers and friends in and out of the house all day. By the end of the day, the entire house looked like a flower shop. We celebrated Christmas with friends and had our Angels for dinner one evening. She got through the holidays with a smile on her face, but when January set in, it became obvious that she was giving up. She'd tell anyone who asked, that although she felt good and it was a beautiful day and she was glad to see them, she was "just sitting here waiting to die." She didn't say this out of depression, just a matter of fact – she couldn't bear the thought of not being productive, of not being able to do the things she loved. Harriet made her a beautiful quilt for her 90th birthday and wrote a very moving letter to go with it. The quilt, she said, was made to accompany Mom on her journey, and for the remaining days in this life, that quilt was never far from her side. That beautiful quilt was placed over her when she went to her final resting place.

Harriet visited us on January 21, 2006. She had a teaching assignment in Phoenix and came in a couple of days early to spend the weekend with Mom. We had a great weekend together – just the three of us – laughing, eating and having fun. Harriet left late Sunday afternoon with the promise that she would be back the following Saturday. She planned to spend Saturday night with us again, before flying home on the following Sunday. It was business as usual on Sunday night when I helped Mama into bed. However, during the night she got sick and never left her bed again. Four days later, on Thursday morning, January 26, at 11:00 AM, my Mama began her next journey. She was in her own home, in her own bed, in no pain, and I was holding her hand as she made the transition to the next stage of her journey.

In the last four days of her life, we spent many hours together, me by her bedside holding her hand and just talking. I was given a gift that most people do not experience. I had four days to say good-bye. We both knew the end was near, although we didn't come right out and say it. She was ready whatever was next. I was not ready to let her go; but there was nothing I could do to stop what she had begun.

Harriet and I were taught that if you have a job to do, you need to get it done. When I got in touch with Harriet on Thursday, she said she was not really surprised. We had talked on Monday evening and I told her that Mama had gotten sick in the night. Knowing that Mama didn't like to be bothered when she wasn't feeling well, Harriet decided to stay with the plan and come back on Saturday after her teaching job was done. On Thursday, we talked about it, and since there were things that I had to do in Phoenix prior to taking Mama on her last trip back to Denver, Harriet finished teaching her classes. Yes, life does go on and I think our ability to finish the job that we started surprised a lot of people. Harriet and I flew to Denver together on Saturday evening, and the following Monday, Mama was laid to rest next to Floyd, her husband, our Father.

Mama had asked me if I planned to remain in our house after she was gone. When I responded yes, the wise woman that was my Mama told me that I had to make our house My home. She said I would not be comfortable living here if I didn't do that very quickly. For the week following my return from Denver, I cleaned, packed, painted, moved furniture and carried out Mom's wishes. The house became My home. Mama's belongings were packed and stored in the garage until Harriet and Carrie could arrange to pick them up. I did not eliminate her presence; I just became the primary resident. She is, however, still with me. There are days I can feel her, there are times I talk to her as if she's just sitting in her chair. Then there are the days I'm driving down the road, and think to myself, "Wow, that's new. I'll have to remember to tell Mama when I get home." Then I remember that is no longer possible.

I was not sure how I would handle the first year of Mama not being with me. It's been a series of ups and downs, but overall, I've done pretty well. What follows is some of what I have experienced, and why I am convinced that she has not left me.

When we first moved into the house, she planted a barrel cactus in the front yard. Then she read in the paper that there was an iris farm on the west side of Phoenix, and asked me to take her there. When she purchased some iris, I must admit I laughed. I told her that iris didn't belong in the desert, but she won. She spent several days preparing the perfect bed for her iris. In twelve years, neither the cactus, nor the iris ever bloomed. She was terribly frustrated with this chain of events, and I teased her a lot about killing this stuff with kindness. She never gave up hope that one or the other would bloom. After she passed, I didn't pay too much attention to the yard for several months. On the Friday before Mother's Day, I was in the front yard, and was startled to see that there were six big yellow flowers on the top of her barrel cactus. That set me back a bit, so I went to the back yard, and was elated to find four iris in full bloom. I am convinced that Mama was saying she wasn't done with her garden just yet.

As the holidays approached, I made fudge and divinity, and felt her on my shoulder every step of the way. Both batches of candy turned out perfect, and I was pretty proud of myself. One evening I was thinking about how good mincemeat cookies would taste. Mincemeat was something else that Mama made from scratch, and I've never tasted any as good as hers. I searched every recipe card I had, and could find nothing in the way of Mama's mincemeat recipe. Putting that idea on the back burner, I decided that after the holidays I'd contact Harriet, and ask her to send a copy of Mama's recipe. Two nights before Christmas, I was thumbing through a recipe book of mine, and what should fall out, but a sheet of paper that had Mama's mincemeat recipe in her handwriting.

Coincidences? Perhaps. I choose to think not. I choose to believe that she's still leaving things for me to find at just the right time in my life. I look forward to the next hide and seek we'll play. I hope it never ends. In this way, Mama will never leave me.

But, there is a hole in my heart now, just as one was formed with the passing of my Father. These are voids that no child can ever fill once their parents are gone. Because I chose the single life – no partner, no children – I often refer to myself as an aging orphan. It can get very lonely at times, but I am blessed with the love and friendship of many people across the country. I will continue to share my message of caregiving and planning for life and the beyond. This has become my passion, and I find it very healing to share Mama's story through my lectures and my writing.

My wish for readers of this book is that you will appreciate not only the hardships, but the love and joy expressed herein. My Mother knew how to make lemonade from lemons, and in her final years she was never irritable, grumpy or otherwise difficult to live with. She was impatient with her limitations, but never with me. She always had a smile on her face for anyone who walked through the door, and she took pleasure in the smallest of things – a bouquet of flowers, the sun shining through the window, one of the cats sitting on her lap. She was truly a remarkable woman and one whose shoes are too big to fill. I only hope that if I reach 90, I can be half the joy to be around that she was.

She had a tendency to cut things out of the newspaper, and stash them away. While going through her desk looking for some family phone numbers, I ran across a poem she had cut out. It was on old, yellow newsprint that was almost brittle. As near as I can tell, she may have found it sometime right after her mother had passed. I was so moved by it, that I asked that it be read at her graveside service. Like I said, there are no coincidences – she meant for me to find this at just the right time. That poem is on the next page.

How is a Mother Remembered?

How is a mother remembered?
Hands busy sewing buttons,
Or dishing up good-smelling things
For hungry little gluttons;

Voice softly humming as she worked
About the house or garden;
The goodnight kiss when you'd been bad
That brought such peace and pardon;

The heavenly smell of homemade bread,
Its warm, moist, special goodness;
The disapproving look when you
Were guilty of some rudeness.

A row of plants upon the sill,
With such care watched and tended;
And stacks of underwear and sox
All neatly darned and mended;

The bedtime stories, and the fun
Of teasing for another -
So many little things make
The memory of Mother.

- Author unknown

Fran's Favorite Candy Recipes

For those of you who have never made cooked candy, the following comments may seem a bit strange. For those of you who have made cooked candy, you will understand.

- ♦ Never attempt to make candy on a cloudy day. Sugar cooks at different rates depending on the atmosphere and the humidity, and your candy will not set if it is cloudy, raining, or anything other than a bright sunny day.

- ♦ An aluminum cook pan works best for candy making. There's something about the even heating process of aluminum that is more effective than stainless steel.

- ♦ Do not use a non-stick pan for fudge. You will beat the candy in the pan and will quickly ruin a non-stick pan with an electric mixer.

- ♦ And last but not least, if your first, tenth or one hundredth try at candy-making results in a mixture that does not set, never, never throw it away. It tastes just as good eaten with a spoon. I've eaten many batches of fudge with a spoon, or spooned into paper candy cups.

Fran's Recipe for Chocolate Fudge

2 cups granulated sugar	1 Tablespoon light corn syrup
1 Tablespoon flour	4 Tablespoons cocoa powder
2/3 cup milk	1 Tablespoon butter
1 Tablespoon vanilla extract	½ cup chopped nuts (optional)

When measuring, exact, level measures are essential. Mix sugar, flour and cocoa powder. Add milk and corn syrup. Cook over medium heat, stirring until the sugar is dissolved. Cook to soft ball stage or about 230 degrees on a candy thermometer. Remove from heat. Place pan in sink with cold water and cool. Add butter and vanilla. If desired, add chopped nuts. With electric mixer, beat until mixture loses its gloss. Pour into an 8" x 8" buttered pan. When candy has set, cut into squares.

Fran's Recipe for Divinity

3 cups granulated sugar   2 egg whites stiffly beaten
¾ cup water   1 Tablespoon vanilla extract
¾ cup light corn syrup   1 cup chopped nuts (optional)

Combine sugar, syrup and water. Bring to a boil stirring until sugar is dissolved. Cook to hard ball stage or 260 degrees on a candy thermometer. While this mixture is cooking, beat egg whites with a stand-mixer. When sugar mixture reaches desired temperature, remove from the heat and very slowly pour into the egg whites while the mixer is running at medium-high to high speed. Continue beating mixture until it stands in stiff peaks and loses its gloss. Add nuts if desired. Pour into a 6" x 9" buttered pan. Let cool and set, then cut into pieces.

My Wish For You

May your own journey be filled with many memories, joy and love. May you always make perfect candy, and have fresh flowers to smell. May you be filled with warm, loving memories of those who have gone on. May you be as blessed as I have been, and continue to be.

Fran's Family Tree

Father			Mother
Frank Abel Carey			Harriet Affie (Williams) Carey
Born September 16, 1871			Born March 20, 1871
Died January 23, 1944			Died January 4, 1954

Sisters	Born	Died	Married
Mabel Helen	January 15, 1902	April 3, 1988	Eugene Kurtz
Gladys Orvetta	March 27, 1903	Dec. 13, 1999	Lloyd Hettinger
Mary Agnes	October 23, 1904	July 1, 1983	Jim Stuart
Ruth Blake	Sept. 18, 1905	Nov. 1, 1993	Milo Johnson
Blanche Elaine	Sept. 19, 1907	Jan. 20, 2004	John Applegate
Sarah Elizabeth	June 10, 1910	Nov. 7, 1988	Cliff Eisiminger
Rowena Maxine	July 2, 1913	Oct. 16, 1999	DeLose Rouse

Harriet Frances (Fran) Carey Frazier
Born December 15, 1915, in Downs, Kansas
Married Floyd Keith Frazier, January 30, 1938
Died January 26, 2006

Husband
Floyd Keith Frazier
Born September 24, 1914, in Portis, Kansas
Married January 30, 1938
Died September 14, 1969, in Denver, Colorado

Daughters

Linda Sue (Frazier) Thompson	Harriet Jane (Frazier)Hargrave
Born: February 22, 1948	Born: October 2, 1952
in Hutchinson, Kansas	in Osborne, Kansas

Granddaughter
Caroline Frances Hargrave
Born: June 19, 1976
In Denver, Colorado

About Linda S. Thompson

Linda Thompson is the founder and president of *Life Path Solutions, Inc.,* a family consulting firm with special emphasis on caregiver issues. For over five years, Linda has facilitated life planning and elder care workshops for corporate employees searching for information, education and resources. Her experience in this arena gave her the boost to write *Planning for Tomorrow, Your Passport to a Confident Future.*

The success of this book led to more speaking opportunities, seminars and workshops. *Planning for Tomorrow* focused on the need for life planning on the non-financial side, as well as the financial and legal necessities. However, no matter the subject of her talk, the questions most often heard were about elder care. Questions such as, "What do I do when Mom can no longer live alone?" "How do I cope with a full time job, a spouse, family and the added responsibility of Dad who is no longer able to make rational decisions?" "How do I gently tell my mother-in-law that she should no longer be driving?"

Linda has had over ten years of walking in a working caregiver's shoes. Because she had done the research, talked to the professionals, and learned the hard way, she soon became the one to call on when someone had an elder care question. Since so many of her clients have expressed having feelings of depression, isolation, and health-related problems associated with being a caregiver, Linda undertook the task of putting common sense suggestions and practical advice into her book, *A Caregiver's Journey, You Are Not Alone.*

There are hundreds of books on the shelves about caregiving. What sets *A Caregiver's Journey* apart is Linda's conversational style of writing, her inclusion of some off-beat humor and some very profound quotes. Her sensible, no-nonsense advice makes this book an easy-to-read, easy-to-use resource for anyone who is (or soon will be) a caregiver.

Linda's mother, Fran, was the catalyst for Linda's journey into the world of elder care. She had been the motivation for Linda's need to learn as much as possible about the aging process and quality of life at the end of the journey. They shared a home for over ten years, and Fran had generously consented to share her journey with others in this book. Linda freely admits that, "Without Mom, my business, my books, and my career would not be possible." Fran began her journey into eternal life on January 26, 2006, two hours after seeing the press proof of this book.

Linda serves on the Board of Directors of the Caregivers Resource Institute, a nonprofit organization dedicated to providing education and information to caregivers. She is a member of the Alliance for Holistic Aging, the National Association of Women Writers, eWomenNetwork, and the American Business Women's Association. Linda lives in Chandler, Arizona with her two cats, Sam and Ginger.

Author's Note

I had no idea that I would be putting the final touches on this manuscript on the one-year anniversary of Mama's passing. When I woke up that morning, I felt a sense of peace and purpose - that she was telling me what I needed to do. I spent ten straight hours at my computer completing Fran's Story. This is what she would have wanted, and it has helped me tremendously.

Books and Tapes Order Form

To order additional copies of *Fran's Story*, or any of Linda's other products, please complete the information below:

Ship to: (please print)

Name: _____

Address: _____

City/State/Zip:_____

Day Phone: _____

E-Mail Address: _____

Product	Qty.	@Price	@Tax*	@S&H	Total
Fran's Story - book		$15.00	$1.56	$5.00**	
A Caregiver's Journey - book		$15.00	$1.56	$5.00**	
Planning for Tomorrow - book		$15.00	$1.56	$5.00**	
Special Offer – All three books		$40.00	$3.12	$7.00**	
Your Safety Net for Life Workbook		$45.00	$3.51	$7.00**	
Family Papers Organizer Data CD		$10.00	$0.78	$1.50	
A Caregiver's Journey-Lecture CD		$10.00	$0.78	$1.50	
Your Safety Net for Life-Lecture CD		$10.00	$0.78	$1.50	
Fran's Story The Final Years CD		$10.00	$0.78	$1.50	

* Arizona Residents Only
** Will ship via USPS Priority Mail

Total Amount enclosed $ _____

Make checks payable to: ***Life Path Solutions, Inc.***

Mail to: Life Path Solutions, Inc.
             2487 S. Gilbert Rd., #106
             Gilbert, AZ 85296-5802

To pay by Visa or MasterCard, please visit our website at
www.LifePathSolutions.biz.
Bulk orders may be ordered at a discounted rate.
For details, please call 1-888-202-9654.

Printed in the United States
80242LV00003B/253-300